In the Land of

SILVER

200 Years of Argentine
Political-Economic Development

Walter Thomas Molano

To Collin
My Little Boy

Chapters

Acknowledgments

Writing is a solitary odyssey that can take your mind far afield and bring you in contact with the most colorful personalities. For almost six months, I journeyed to the vast halls of Sterling Memorial Library at Yale University to encounter the various characters that constructed the history of Argentina. Each day, different episodes of the country's development came to life beneath the vaulted arches of the Starr Reference Room. I am very grateful to the library staff members who made my work possible and who compensated for my woeful lack of a research assistant. I next salute the scholars and academics who guided me. Ricardo Lopez Murphy, one of the greatest economists in Argentina, was essential in piecing together the vast domestic literature on the country's economic development. The same is true for Erik Wibbels of Duke University, who provided me with valuable insights into the growing field of political and economic geography. Likewise, Carlos Carballo, Julio Nogues, and

Fernando del Corro were essential in navigating the nuances of the country's history. I would like to thank former Economy Minister Roberto Lavagna for taking time out of his hectic schedule to retell some of his experiences. Finally, my old dissertation-committee friend, John Aldrich, opened my eyes to the great advances in publishing manuscripts.

I next acknowledge the people who took the time and patience to read the manuscript. First, and foremost, I thank my wife, Mary Beth. Her patience and words of encouragement kept me going through the difficult patches. Next, I thank Gonzalo de Castro, Mariano Kruskevich, Manuel Lopez Delagar, and Ken Tolo who took the time to correct my mistakes and misconceptions.

Last of all, I thank my family for putting up with my long absences and endless pondering as the tale of Argentina's history wove through my mind.

Prologue

Argentina vexes. It is a huge landmass with abundant natural wealth and a sophisticated population. Argentina is the eighth largest country in the world, roughly a third of the continental United States. If it were superimposed over the North American landmass, it would stretch from Cuba to the middle of the Hudson Bay in Canada. It is endowed with a bounty of resources, including excellent topsoil, an abundance of fresh water, and a wide diversity of fauna. It is also blessed with a well-educated work force. At the turn of the twentieth century, millions of European immigrants escaping political and religious persecution fled to Argentina; many were escaping the ravages of economic privation as well. This influx of immigrants allowed Argentina initially to follow the path of similarly endowed countries, such as the United States, Canada, and Australia, by developing export-driven sectors that exploited the commodities at their disposal. At the start of the twentieth century, Argentina was one of the wealthiest countries on the planet, with innovative technology and modern armament. Its capital, Buenos Aires, was a beaming metropolis with an excellent metro transport system, Beaux-Arts architecture, and the widest avenues in the world. However, something went awry during the twentieth century that allowed it to lose its way.

The derailment of Argentina has been the topic of countless books, academic papers, and discussions. There have been many explanations, including the form of colonization, the quality of the immigrants who developed the country, and its heavy dependence on agriculture. Some have claimed that Argentina's problems stem from excessive settlement by the Spanish, which left a legacy of mismanagement and deep-seated corruption. Others have pointed to the heavy presence of the Southern Europeans who gave it a Mediterranean flair. This was in contrast to the prominence of Northern Europeans who settled in the United States, Canada, and Australia. At the same time, a large group of development experts attributed Argentina's problems to the dominance of agriculture, which prevented the development of heavy industries. Its reliance on commodities made it vulnerable to sharp swings in external prices and left the economy inherently unstable. All three factors shaped the country's trajectory.

These oversimplifications of the historical record have resulted in unfair prejudices and stereotypes. There are far more examples of failed countries that were once part of Northern European empires. The Congo, Haiti, and Rwanda are not held up as shining examples of enlightened development despite their control by Belgium, France, and Germany.

The United Kingdom particularly gets high marks for its exemplary administration of colonial states. The United States, Canada, and Australia are displayed as showcases of proper colonial management as well. Meanwhile, the Spanish are said to have left a wasteland of failed colonies across much of Latin America, Africa, and Asia. What explains the divergence? Anglophiles highlight English jurisprudence, Lockean divisions of power, and the Protestant work ethic. At the same time, Spanish corruption and Catholicism seem to have been their colonies' downfall. It is true that the Spanish traditions of absolutism contrasted heavily with England's constitutional monarchy. The latter allowed for a more representative form of government. Meanwhile, the former amplified bad policy decisions by not allowing a system of checks and balances. Yet, does the historical record support the claims that the British crown left a better legacy of successful colonies?

A closer look at the evidence reveals that England also left its fair share of developmental disasters. Sub-Saharan Africa, the Middle East, and the Caribbean have plenty of failed states that flew the Union Jack. Moreover, Britain's experience in India was more in line with Spain's encounter with Latin America. Replete with viceroys and British-born overlords, the colonial system was established to administer a very large population without any intention of integrating them or giving them a representative voice. One could even argue that the subcontinent's immense potential is being actualized despite its British colonial legacy. Most of the social woes that still plague India are the direct result of British rule. A policy of divide and conquer laid waste to centuries of social harmony and diversity. The country's economic might emanates from its huge population base and its pre-colonial traditions that emphasized innovation and education.

So, what explains the few triumphal colonies that were established by the British? The most successful cases are stories of extermination and displacement rather than assimilation and domination. The common denominator between Australia, the United States, and Canada is that they were societies that displaced the native populations through wars of annihilation. In essence, they used genocidal methods to sweep away indigenous groups in order to make room for the new colonists. As a result, there was no need to integrate the natives. There was no existence of a subclass with a different culture and without the skills needed to move up the social ladder.

At the same time, the Spanish colonies were extractive operations that used the local population as the main source of labor. The organizational structure was based on the *encomiendo* (meaning *to take charge*) system, whereby colonists were assigned groups of natives. In other words, the colonists were responsible for the welfare of the indigenous people group while the crown retained title and ownership to much of the land—particularly the subsoil and mineral rights. This allowed the monarch to become a profit-maximizing agent instead of a provider of public goods, such as law and order. The colonists were regarded almost as employees in a vast business venture. This arrangement was accentuated by the fact that the colonists did not pay any royal taxes. Tax collection was purely for local administration. Not surprisingly, the complaints of taxation without representation were absent in the Spanish colonies. Therefore, the system was an autocratic structure that used coercion, both physical and religious, to control a very large population with no intent to integrate it or give it a greater voice in government. Unfortunately, this left several sad institutional legacies that persist to this day. It created a large underclass with almost no chance of upward social mobility. It also left a society with no tradition of representative government.

In the same way that the qualities of the colonizing nations did not have much of an effect on postcolonial performance, the patterns of immigration were also inconsequential. The United States, Canada, and Australia received as many Southern and Eastern European immigrants as Argentina. They brought their cultures and traditions, which are still proudly displayed across cities such as Toronto, New York, and Sydney. Individuals of Italian, Russian, and Polish descent rose to prominence and sometimes to infamy in all three countries. Likewise, there was a great deal of assimilation into the local culture. Immigrants to Argentina took great pride in their new homeland and embraced the language, religion, and traditions of Latin America. Today, Argentines of Welsh, Jewish, and Basque descent are fully integrated as pure locals, just as their cousins are ingrained into North American and Australian life. Therefore, the pattern of immigration has very little to do with any nation's path of development other than to create silly stereotypes.

Last of all, the initial economic successes of the United States, Canada, and Australia were primarily due to their role as major commodity producers. These three countries have huge land-masses that bristle with an abundance of natural resources. Their populations are also relatively small in proportion to their land-masses. Therefore, they have excess supplies of raw materials that can be easily dispatched to other parts of the world. Indeed, cotton was the main US export until the early part of the twentieth century. It was not until the heavy industrialization brought about by the Second World War that the United States transformed itself into a manufacturing economy. Given the destruction and devastation that occurred across most of Europe and Asia during that conflict, the United States remained as the major source of manufactured goods for the next two decades. It was not until the late 1960s and early 1970s when the Germans and Japanese were able to get back on their feet that the United States returned to its commodity roots. Canada and Australia remained closely tied to their areas of comparative advantage. That is why their economic cycles are similar to Argentina's, though perhaps with smaller swings in amplitude. Nevertheless, these two countries suffer whenever commodity prices drop, and they prosper whenever commodities rally. Therefore, Argentina's development record has not been merely a function of its basic economic model. It has been driven by other factors.

So, if Argentina's pattern of economic development has not been due to the nature of its colonizers, the composition of its immigrants, or the structure of its exports, then what explains its record? It is clear that these factors played some role, but there had to be other endogenous and exogenous explanations. I believe that very little emphasis has been placed on the uniqueness of Argentina's geography and the role it played. Understanding Argentina's location, topography, and physical attributes provides enormous insights into the path the country has taken since colonization, its current role in the global context, and its opportunities for the future.

Very little is written about the effect a country's geography has on its history and development. Geography is considered a random set of factors that are exploited, abused, or ignored. Nevertheless, land, along with labor and capital, was one of the three factors of production delineated by Adam Smith. Unfortunately, economists are more interested in studying the contribution of labor and capital to total factor productivity since these can be much more dynamically combined. Land, or geography, is a passive factor. Nevertheless, it shapes decisions by limiting or expanding the range of options that are available to the population and policymakers.

When Argentina was a marginal outpost of the Spanish Empire, it was considered an empty wasteland bereft of the mineral riches that abounded in Alto Peru and the Sierra Madre. Nevertheless, its proximity to the mines of Potosi and the deep river system that drained the *altiplano* made it a very interesting location at the turn of the nineteenth century. Likewise, the vast expanses of fertile topsoil gave it an enviable advantage when new technologies were developed to facilitate the transportation of agricultural goods.

The history of Argentina is molded by its land. Its geography is deeply etched in the Argentine psyche, and it is what allows the nation to play such an important role on the international stage. The ability of its population to harness its natural resources has allowed it to recover quickly and repeatedly from bouts of devastating mismanagement and external shocks. This book hopes to provide a better understanding of this austral country that seems to be so sequestered from other nations that are similar in size and import. I intend to delve deep into the historical record in order to highlight the pivotal events that have sculpted the formation of the nation. My intent is to go well beyond the single-dimensional caricatures that are often used to paint developing countries. In the process, we will see that Argentina is one of the more interesting and complex societies of the developing world.

Geographical and Colonial Legacies

Argentina's geography is fascinating. In addition to sheer beauty, it is vast. With half of the landmass of the continental United States, Argentina has only 15 percent of its population. Thousands of square miles of glaciers provide it with one of the largest sources of fresh water on the planet. An extensive river system stretches deep into the hinterland, endowing it with a network of navigable waterways. It has huge expanses of arable land with thick topsoil that is rich in nutrients. Its oil and natural gas deposits are immense, and the Andean mountains are chocked with minerals. Ancient forests in the south are an important source of wood and timber, and the nitrate fields of the northern deserts contain some of the largest sediments of lithium salts in the world. Its massive deposits of rare earth minerals rival those found in China. To say the least, Argentina is endowed with a cornucopia of wealth.

Argentina's long, narrow landmass stretches from the tropics to the Antarctic, but its temperature is moderated by the ocean that delineates the coastline. The temperate climate is complemented by two permanent weather patterns. The northern part of the country is covered by the southeasterly trade winds that carry a great deal of humidity from the Atlantic. The southwestern region is soaked by the prevailing westerly winds that carry rain from the Pacific. These patterns ensure an annual rainfall of twenty inches per year over more than 40 percent of the landmass. In addition to the generous rainfall, the long stretch of the snow-covered Andes provides ample sources of riverine flow.[1]

The immense power produced by the Parana River is also an important source of energy. It is tapped by the Yacyereta and Itapúa Dams, both of which are part of the generation capacity that feeds much of the industrial strength of northern Argentina, thus allowing the various factories in Santa Fe, Cordoba, and the Province of Buenos Aires to thrive. At the same time, large hydroelectric complexes along the Andes power the agro-industrial activities of the Pampas and southern Argentina. In a world where water is becoming one of the scarcest resources, Argentina enjoys an unrecognized abundance.

The diversity of microclimates throughout the vast country allows a variety of crops and products to be produced. The northern tropical climates of Salta, Corrientes, and Tucuman are conducive to the production of fruits and sugar cane. The

---

1   Bailey Willis, *Northern Patagonia: Character and Resources* (Buenos Aires: Ministry of Public Works, 1914), 2-5.

wet foothills of the Andes, particularly the provinces of Mendoza and San Juan, are well suited for growing grapes. The climates of Salta and Corrientes are ideal for the growing of tobacco. Meanwhile, the vast plains of Cordoba, Santa Fe, and Buenos Aires are perfect for sowing wheat, corn, and soybeans. The extensive pastures of southern Buenos Aires and the province of La Pampa are ideal for cattle, and the scrub land of Patagonia is perfectly suited for sheep. The convergence of the Paraguay and Uruguay Rivers creates a delta that is as large as the Mississippi River Delta with an equal diversity of flora and fauna.

Many other countries share similar climatic conditions. For example, Paraguay has abundant rainfall. The same climate occurs in the plains of Santa Cruz in lower Bolivia as well as on the vast savannah of Mato Grosso in Brazil, but none of these has the same combination of abundant water, rich topsoil, and facile communication with the outside world that Argentina has. Bolivia and Paraguay are landlocked. The rich farmlands of southwestern Brazil are blocked by a series of littoral states that make it virtually impossible to get their products to market, thanks to a Byzantine web of taxes, regulation, and poor infrastructure.

Argentina's geography also provides it with several strategic advantages. The Andes and the frigid waters of the South Atlantic act as natural buffers against foreign invasion. It is located far away from the industrialized world, which acts as a detractor against external intervention.[2] The neighboring

---

2   This is something that the British experienced during the War of the Malvinas in 1982. The British flotilla was forced to sail with a complement of 127 ships, consisting of 43 warships, 22 auxiliary vessels, and 62 merchantmen to supply the distant expedition. Although the British were ultimately victorious, they left many of their newest frigates and destroyers at the bottom of the South Atlantic.

states to the north, such as Bolivia, Paraguay, and Uruguay, are small and do not provide any meaningful threat. Meanwhile, the border with Brazil is narrow and consists of a thinly populated area. Therefore, Argentina is comfortably isolated behind a series of natural boundaries that give it a great deal of security and self-confidence. Although it fought several wars of expansion during the nineteenth and twentieth centuries, it was never forced to resort to heavy military spending in order to defend its frontiers.

Argentina may be a developing nation, but it has a very long history. The first inhabitants arrived well before the end of the Ice Age. Humans penetrated deep into Patagonia, leaving vivid cave drawings along with other vestiges of their civilization. The Cave of Hands in the Province of Santa Cruz is not just important for its antiquity, but for the ingenious use of colors and negative/positive imagery. Prior to the arrival of the first European settlers, most of the region was inhabited by nomadic tribes. The exception was in the northwest, which was at the fringe of the Inca Empire. The Incas penetrated as far south as the Province of Mendoza where the ruins of Shinkal are still visible. They left a large population in the region of Cuyo along the foothills of the Andes. Unfortunately, most of the inhabitants in the remainder of the country succumbed to European diseases, or they were slaughtered in military campaigns. Therefore, Argentina's native legacies are few. This is in contrast with Peru, Bolivia, and Mexico where there is a strong cultural presence of earlier civilizations.

The colonial history of Argentina began in 1580 when Juan de Garay, the military governor of Asuncion, established a permanent military base on the southern bank of the River

Plate. He explored the estuary of the Parana and Paraguay Rivers,[3] but most of his expeditions were in the headlands of those two waterways because they were suitable locations for the fortifications of Santa Cruz and Santa Fe. It is important to note that despite the River Plate's access to the Atlantic, the exploration of the territory was made from the north. The conquest of the continent was organized from the Spanish garrisons in Peru. This helped give the colony its northern orientation, always leaving the south as a desolate frontier. De Garay and his men were not seeking new lands for habitation. They were veterans of the wars against the Moors and soldiers of fortune in search of loot and conquest. When they failed to find precious metals to steal or populations to enslave, they moved on. Unfortunately, the legacies of these rough military men helped shape the political institutions of the colony.

Indeed, the unification of Spain was a pivotal moment in American and European history. Most people consider the conquest of the Moors a coincidental backdrop to Columbus's voyages of discovery. However, the context of the crossing was just as important as the journey itself. On January 2, 1492, King Boabdil surrendered Granada after an eighteen-month siege by a Catholic army of eighty thousand men, thus ending eight hundred years of Islamic presence on the Iberian Peninsula. The conquest was a testament to the Catholic kings' shrewd maneuvering, ruthless determination, and exploitation of the political divisions among the Moors. Al-Andalus was an open society that extended religious tolerance to Christians and Jews. The atmosphere of *convivencia*,

---

3   Actually, this was the second founding of Buenos Aires. The first one occurred in 1536 by Pedro de Mendoza, but it was destroyed by the natives.

or coexistence, allowed cities such as Toledo, Cordoba, and Granada to flourish into bastions of science and technology by preserving and translating many of the texts of the ancient world. They also pushed out the frontiers of knowledge through rigorous research and scholarship. Yet, Al-Andalus was deeply divided due to rivalry, jealously, and hatred. By the end of the eleventh century, it was partitioned into twenty-three separate city-states. The Moorish rulers often enlisted the help of Christian mercenaries and monarchs in their battles against each other. As a result, the states were vulnerable and thus easy marks during the reconquest of the Iberian Peninsula.

This strategy of divide and conquer was used repeatedly by the Spanish during the subjugation of the Americas. Such Machiavellian tactics allowed them to overcome superior numbers through guile and deceit. The Spanish consolidated their control through religion and social division, which is how they subverted the population after the fall of Al-Andalus. There was no such thing as honor among the conquistadores, and most promises were broken as soon as they were sealed. The ruthless tactics that proved to be so successful on the Iberian plain turned out to be equally effective in the sierras and jungles of the New World.

The discovery of the Americas was timely. Spain was a backwater of ignorance and poverty at the end of the 1400s. Centuries of endless battles had depleted government coffers. The monarchy needed to develop new sectors of economic activity rather than rely on fighting and looting to stay flush with capital. The arid plains of Iberia were bereft of the agricultural bounty that was found across the Pyrenees. The Romans had depleted much of the mineral resources that were once abundant, such as gold and silver. The Spaniards, like many other Europeans, envied the rich kingdoms of the eastern Mediterranean where the crossroads of Europe, Asia, and Africa came together to create one of the largest bazaars in the world. The so-called Silk Road created vast fortunes for the merchants of the Byzantine states. Constantinople, indeed, was the gateway to Asia. Several European city-states developed lucrative trading relationships, and the cities of Constantinople, Venice, Genoa, and Florence emerged as the major powers of the central Mediterranean. The trade surpluses produced by these Italian city-states allowed them to accumulate the resources needed to finance the revival of the arts and sciences that flourished during the Renaissance.

The obsession with Asia explained why Portugal tried so hard to circumvent the Mediterranean by developing an alternate trade route around Africa. During the first half of the fifteenth century, Henry the Navigator established a school near Sagres that allowed his country to become a major sea power. Using Islamic navigation instruments, maps, and sailing practices, his students were able to venture far from shore. The information was so secret that Portuguese naval officers were threatened with death if they revealed any of their navigation techniques.[4] Holland also tried to find an alternate route to Asia, sending men and ships above Scandinavia and Russia. Unfortunately, they were blocked by ice and the large archipelago of Nova Zembla.

It was within this setting that a certain Genovese navigator offered his services to the Spanish monarchs in order to find a new route to the Indies by cutting across the Atlantic. In

---

4   Aldo Ferrer, La Economía Argentina: Desde sus Orígenes hasta los Principios del Siglo XXI (Buenos Aires: Fondo de Cultura Económica, 2004), 21.

contrast to the myth that the world was flat, medieval scholars knew that the planet was spherical.[5] The ludicrous notion
of the flat world was invented by Washington Irving, the errant
American who penned "The Legend of Sleepy Hollow" and
"Rip Van Winkle." Irving spent several years in Spain writing
about the conquest of the Moors and the life of Christopher
Columbus. Nevertheless, he was more of a romantic than
a scholar. The Medieval academics who were consulted on
Columbus's proposition advised against the venture because
his calculations were off, and they knew that he would run
out of supplies before he reached his destination. They were
right. Just as he was running out of provisions, he made landfall. However, he did not arrive in Asia. He came ashore in the
New World.

Yet, why were the Catholic monarchs willing to take
a bet on such a reckless undertaking? The answer is that
desperate situations often induce people to make very risky
bets. They simply had nothing to lose because much of the
Mediterranean was already blocked by Islamic pirates. The
Venetians and Genovese also guarded their trade routes jealously. Therefore, trade with the eastern Mediterranean was
virtually impossible, and the Spanish monarchs needed an
alternate route to the east. Columbus's venture was bold.
He had already secured some funding from Italian investors.
Although they never gained any of the lands that were discovered in the New World, the Italians were major patrons of
the voyages of exploration. The Medicis, for example, spec-
ulated heavily in Henry the Navigator's school and various
adventures. The Spanish monarchs were also enjoying the

---

5   The Greek astronomer Eratosthenes made the first accurate measurement of the Earth's
circumference in 240 BC.

windfall associated with the conquest of Granada. Although the Moors were allowed to leave with their possessions, their lands were passed on to the crown. Therefore, the monarchs were flush with cash, and they were able to afford a risky bet. Still, it is important to stress that Columbus's voyage was never done for conquest, colonization, or glory. It was purely a commercial undertaking.

For the next two decades, the project did not produce any meaningful gains. It took the explorers several years before they realized that they had not disembarked in the Indies. Instead, they had alighted in a totally unknown continent. Hence, the idea of finding a new route to Asia went up in smoke, and there was only the hope that they could find some loot to help compensate for their losses. Unfortunately, things didn't look too promising. The explorers returned to the Old World with new fruits and vegetables, and with a few indigenous people as well. Corn, tomatoes, and chilies were some of the plants they brought back with them. There was some gold, but it was not until the conquest of the Aztecs by Hernan Cortes in 1521 that the outlook for the enterprise improved. Cortes was a heartless mercenary, and he used many of the traitorous tactics that had been employed against the Moors. He used a series of lies, kidnappings, and extortions to conquer the indigenous people. He exploited rivalries between elements of the Aztec empire and formed temporary alliances to overcome superior forces. In the end, his rabble of desperate men was able to defeat one of the most sophisticated civilizations on the planet.

Although Columbus did not find a new route to Asia, the discovery of the Americas played an important role in bridging the two continents. Europeans had always had a deep affinity for Asian wares. The East has a long history of manufacturing and technology. The West's obsession with Chinese porcelains and silks goes back thousands of years. India developed sophisticated techniques to weave cotton into cloth well before the birth of Christ. It was the demand for these products that drove the explorers to find new trade routes to the Indies. Unfortunately, the Europeans did not have much to barter in exchange. Europe was just emerging from the Dark Ages, and the quality of its products was extremely low. The Asians were happy to receive bullion in exchange for their goods, but the Europeans did not have much to offer. As mentioned before, the Romans had already exhausted most of Europe's silver and gold. Some scholars even attribute the downfall of the Roman Empire to the massive depletion of reserves used to pay for Asian imports.[6] That is why the discovery of silver and gold in the Americas was so important to the Europeans; it gave them bartering power.

Twelve years after Cortes subjugated the Aztecs, Francisco Pizzaro's mob of conquistadores overran the Inca Empire through superior firepower, chicanery, and duplicity. Like Cortes, Pizzaro hailed from the hardscrabble region of Extramadura. In 1533, he invaded the Inca Empire and treacherously executed its monarch, and in the process of doing so, he decapitated the nation's political leadership. Like the Aztecs, the Incas had developed a sophisticated technology to smelt precious metals and manufacture goods with them. They panned the rivers for gold flakes and used mining techniques to extract silver. They then used complex molds to create delicate ornaments. The first shipments of

---

6   Susan Whitfield with Ursula Sims-Williams, eds., *The Silk Route: Trade, Travel, War and Faith* (London: British Library, 2004).

bullion sent to Spain were comprised of objects that had been looted from the Indians. The Spanish colonists subsequently set out to find more sources of precious metals. They hit pay dirt when they found the mines of Potosi more than two thousand kilometers from Lima in a barren stretch of the Peruvian altiplano. The Cerro Rico mine turned out to be one of the largest silver deposits in the world. More than forty-five thousand tons of silver were dug out of its shafts, and it provided the bulk of the bullion that flowed into Europe for the next two centuries.

Initially, the silver wound its way through Europe in a serpentine trail of transactions before making its way to the East. However, at the end of the sixteenth century, a more direct route between the Americas and Asia was established. In 1571, Miguel López de Legazpi occupied Manila and formally established Spain's presence in Asia. In contrast with the American colonies, Manila was used as a transshipment center to facilitate commerce with China and the other Asian markets. The trade route with Mexico brought Asian products directly to the American colonists in exchange for silver. Given that there were no precious metals or minerals to be mined in the Philippines, the Spanish authorities had no interest in subjugating the local population. Instead, the Catholic Church was given the primary role of maintaining religious, social, and political order, thus developing a very heavy influence over everyday life. This is still evident today.[7]

---

7   The heavy trade between the Philippines and New Spain allowed the two colonies to develop deep cultural ties that are still visible today. Asian porcelain vases are a prevalent feature in Mexican décor, and Spanish cooking techniques are permanent features of Filipino cuisine. Unfortunately, the trade between the two colonies also led to a serious depletion of bullion and reserves, forcing the authorities to clamp down on trans-Pacific trade.

The importance of the mining operations soon defined how the colonies were organized. The extraction of minerals became the overriding objective of the colonial system, followed by the control of the indigenous population and the state's monopolization of trade. This forced the Spaniards to reorganize their institutions into a mercantilist system, thus allowing the crown to maximize revenues. The regions with the highest concentrations of precious metals became the centers of attention. In order to administer the operations, the government set up the viceroyalty system, which was led by a viceroy who served as the king's direct proxy. This was an institutional arrangement that had been developed by the Kingdom of Aragon when it administered the islands of Corsica and Sardinia during the fourteenth century.

The first viceroyalty was established in 1535. New Spain constituted much of present-day Mexico and Central America. This was followed by the Viceroyalty of Peru in 1542, which was responsible for most of South America. The third colonial headquarters was not established until 1717 when the northern part of South America was separated into the Viceroyalty of Nueva Granada. It was established to provide direct control over present-day Venezuela, Colombia, and Ecuador. The discovery of large gold deposits in Antioquia and Choco brought the region into the royal spotlight, and the Spanish authorities felt that the operations needed direct oversight from Madrid.

The viceroyalties were complemented by smaller autonomous regions called captaincies. Chile and the Philippines were two such examples. Although government ministers in Spain dictated general policies dealing with trade and mining, the colonists were given a great deal of discretion in local affairs. Local government was administered by a *cabildo* comprised of business owners, members of the clergy, and military men. They directed the crown's edicts and established militias to ensure public control and the defense against indigenous or slave uprisings. In order to ensure loyalty to the authorities in Spain, only native-born Spaniards or *peninsulares* were allowed to hold important public positions. Initially, this condition seemed logical, but as time wore on and generations of creoles gained wealth and power, it became a cause of disagreement.

In order for the crown to maximize its control over the mines, it appointed itself the sole proprietor of mineral and subsoil property rights. The colonists were put in charge of the indigenous population employed to work the mines. As detailed earlier, this was known as the *encomiendo* system, whereby the monarchy entrusted the colonists with the physical and spiritual well-being of the local population. In return, they could use the natives as they saw fit.[8]

Control of the population was one of the most important challenges faced by the Spanish colonists. Rather than extermination—a practice that was common in North America and Australia—the objective was domination. As we saw in the case of the Philippines, the Spanish employed two important techniques to govern such large groups. The first was religion. Most of the major Catholic orders, such as the Dominicans, Jesuits, and Franciscans, were given responsibilities over large

---

8   The organizational relationship between the state and the creoles became a permanent feature of the Spanish colonial system and a powerful legacy in the development of Latin American economies. Although the state owned the major productive assets, the private sector acted as providers and suppliers—thus allowing them to enjoy a very lucrative arrangement. This symbiotic relationship, unfortunately, was highly inefficient because it was focused on maintaining loyalty between the government and the private sectors.

territories. In order to fully achieve their objective, the Church also deployed the Inquisition—a tool that was very successful in rooting out seditious elements after the conquest of the Moors. The second tool was the use of the caste system. The population was finely segmented with the *peninsulares* at the top of the hierarchy and the slaves at the bottom. In between was a wide range of castes that included freed slaves, indentured workers, Indians, mestizos, and creoles. Thus, a small group of Spaniards was able to control an overwhelmingly large population by seeding dissent and resentment among the various classes and by dispensing privileges and obligations at will. These same tactics had proved very effective in dominating the Moors by segmenting the society into *conversos*, *moriscos*, and *maranos*.

Initially, the colonial economies were rudimentary. Most transactions were in the form of barter. However, as the mining operations flourished, the colonists demanded imported goods. The problem was that all international trade was the purview of the monarch and thus subject to taxation. This was one of the main sources of government revenue. In addition to tariffs, the Spanish monarchy also established the terms and conditions of trade, which allowed them to justify the full use of mercantilism. The administrative center of the colonial trading system was the Casa de Contratacion in Seville, which was situated on the Guadalquivir River eighty kilometers from the coast. Therefore, it was safe to unload the treasure ships that arrived from the Americas and reload them with wares for the return journey.

Although a constant stream of ships plied the oceans, large convoys of about two dozen ships were sent twice a year. Both fleets made landfall in Cartagena, but one would then set out for Veracruz with wares destined for Central America and Mexico. The other would continue on to Porto Bello, where the merchandise would be shipped over the Isthmus of Panama and redirected toward the ports of Lima, Arica, and Guayaquil. The initial markup on the merchandise was 100 to 300 percent, but it could reach 700 to 1,000 percent by the time it reached the miners of Potosi. In addition to licensing all merchandise for trade with the Americas, the Casa de Contratacion also enforced commercial laws and regulations, and collected custom duties. Therefore, it was the political and the administrative center for colonial matters.

It was against the backdrop of mining and highly controlled trade that the small outpost of Buenos Aires flourished as an important hub for contraband. By the early part of the eighteenth century, Potosi had become one of the richest cities on the planet. The miners hosted sumptuous balls and squandered money recklessly. It was said that women would order the latest fashions from Paris only to wear them once and throw them away. Like the Mexican colonists who hungered for Asian wares, the miners of Potosi clamored for luxury goods from Europe, including furnishings, clothes, and books. Despite their immense wealth, the colonists soon found that goods smuggled from Buenos Aires were six to eight times less expensive than those sold through official channels.[9] Part of the reason for the discrepancy was the shorter distance those goods traveled. The European merchandise that entered the country through the official route had to travel the lengthy voyage across the Atlantic, through the jungles of Panama, and back down the Pacific,

---

9 Aldo Ferrer, La Economía Argentina: Desde sus Orígenes hasta los Principios del Siglo XXI (Buenos Aires: Fondo de Cultura Económica, 2004), 67.

thus involving a long list of middlemen. The contraband that entered through Buenos Aires, however, arrived after a much shorter transatlantic crossing and fewer intermediaries. At the same time, the travel times between the two ports of entry were very different. The transit time between Buenos Aires and Potosi was only two months, but the travel time between Lima and Potosi was twice as long.

Not only was the distance from Buenos Aires shorter; it was easier to transport from there because of the river system. Merchants could sail their cargos up the Parana and Paraguay Rivers to the foothills of the Andes and complete the last part of the journey by mule. This helped reduce costs. Lastly, the monopolistic powers of the official channel allowed government agents to mark up prices with abandon. Meanwhile, the merchants who sold into the markets of Buenos Aires had to compete against one another. This transformed Buenos Aires into the main conduit of smuggled goods that penetrated deep into the heart of the Spanish Empire. So much bullion flowed out of the estuary that it became known as the River of Silver, Rio de la Plata, which is translated into English as the River Plate. The country even came to be known as the land of silver—Argentina.

It is here that geography played a crucial role. Buffeted by Brazil to the east—a land that was occupied by unfriendly Portuguese—and the rugged Andes to the north and west, the rivers became the easiest way for the miners to gain access to the outside world, which made Buenos Aires the only entry point for the entire Spanish-controlled region. This was in contrast to other littoral colonies during the colonial period that had a variety of ports, such as New York, Boston, Philadelphia, and Charleston in North America. However, this was not the case with the settlements of the River Plate. The southernmost ports of present-day Argentina, such as Bahia Blanca, Mar del Plata, and Puerto Madryn, were virtually impossible to reach. They were a very far distance to travel to, and were surrounded by inhospitable deserts and hostile natives. Thus, Buenos Aires was the only oceanic access point for the trading communities that developed along the outskirts of Potosi. Many of the provinces had riverine ports, but all of these waterways converged just before the shores of Buenos Aires, which meant the powerbrokers of that city were able to control everything that entered and exited the region. This is why it emerged as the natural center of trade, contraband, and eventually, colonial administration.

Buenos Aires became such an important center of contraband that the crown decided to bring it under military control in 1776 by creating the Viceroyalty of the River Plate. Under the colonial system of administration, all operating costs were subtracted from revenues before they were remitted to Spain. Given the high costs of importing goods and materials across the official channels, the operational efficiency of the Potosi mines was in a permanent state of decline. Colonial administrators realized that they could maximize their gains by inflating costs. At the same time, many of the mines were being depleted, which meant they had to dig deeper shafts. These new ventures required expensive drainage systems, equipment, and pumps; otherwise, the shafts would flood. With much of the high-grade ore exhausted, the miners began using mercury to extract silver from lower-grade material. The process was dear, since it required large quantities of the liquid metal. Therefore, the Spanish government needed to reduce costs and improve efficiency.

It soon became apparent that one of the ways to reduce expenses was to import all material across the Atlantic to Buenos Aires and up the rivers, thus bypassing Lima. This initiative was vehemently opposed by the viceroy of Peru since it would curtail his territory and income, but the monarchy was desperate for money. Buenos Aires was designated a viceroyalty, and it became the fourth major center of Spanish colonial administration.

Now that it was no longer an outpost of illegal activity, Buenos Aires was transformed into an official center that levied and collected customs on imported merchandise. Contrabandists were reincarnated into official government agents who acted in the interest of the crown. Many of them continued to function in a dual capacity carrying out legitimate transactions while pursuing illegal side deals for their own gain. Unfortunately, the institutionalization of corruption was a tradition that would carry on. Moreover, the geography of the region transformed Buenos Aires into a virtual tollbooth on the River Plate, a role that the city would play for many years, thus keeping it at odds with the rest of the country.

The nature and character of Buenos Aires was quite different from the other viceroyalties. Most of the other colonies were mainly populated by Spaniards, creoles, mestizos, and indigenous peoples. However, Buenos Aires was an eclectic mix of European nationalities. The port and the contraband business attracted a wide array of immigrants who gave the city a much more international setting than the other capitals of the empire. As the city prospered, it developed a network of schools and universities that educated many of the merchants, lawyers, and intellectuals who eventually carried the revolutionary torches of the independence movement.

Initially, Buenos Aires and the provinces were on similar paths. The provincial economies were also by-products of the immense mineral wealth that was generated by Potosi. They provided many of the perishable items needed for everyday life. Given the inhospitable environment of the Peruvian altiplano, the miners needed to find alternate sources for agricultural products. Provinces such as Salta, Tucuman, and Cordoba developed large industrial plantations that provided fruits, vegetables, and beasts of burden. The success of the mining operations during the seventeenth and eighteenth centuries spurred a sharp increase in the numbers of miners, eventually peaking at approximately two hundred thousand. This generated greater demand for supplies. One of the more interesting suppliers that arrived on the scene was the Catholic Church.[10]

During the early part of the seventeenth century, the Jesuits constructed five major plantations in Cordoba to produce wine, vitals, and supplies for the mining operations. They used the profits to fund the local education system for the indigenous population and the centers of higher education for the creoles. The most successful institution to emerge from the system was the University of Cordoba. It is one of the oldest surviving institutions of higher learning in the Americas and one of the best universities in Argentina. The Jesuit plantations thrived for the next century and a half, and the local population and highbred creoles became well educated as a result. Initially, the Jesuits were welcomed. However, their

---

10 The tradition of privileged suppliers providing inflated services to large government commercial operations is a theme that would resonate throughout Argentine history. Many of the richest families established their fortunes by using this symbiotic relationship between the public and private sectors.

shrewd business operations eventually sowed resentment among local merchants.

The economic development of the provinces was slow. The most powerful provincial economic institutions were the plantations, but they were basic organizations that provided workers with room, board, and education in exchange for labor. Very little money was in circulation. Most transactions occurred on a barter basis. This limitation hampered the workers' economic development, since it curtailed the availability of credit, savings, and investment.[11] In contrast, Buenos Aires had a modern economic structure that employed money freely. This attracted investors and speculators, which led to the formation of banks.

The Jesuit missionaries treated the indigenous population better than most groups did in many parts of the empire. They were taught skills that allowed them to become independent artisans. The success of the first missions at the foothills of the Andes led to the proliferation of more plantations farther east along the banks of the Parana River where there was a large Guarani population. Using the proceeds from the plantations, the Jesuits converted thousands of Guarani to Catholicism. However, the missions along the Parana were soon entangled in open conflict with Portuguese slave traders from Brazil.

Although the Portuguese never encountered large organized civilizations in Brazil such as the Incas or Aztecs, they found huge mineral deposits. In the seventeenth century, gold was discovered in Minas Gerais, Goias, and Matto Grosso. However, the Portuguese colonists lacked the labor to exploit

---

11 Roberto Cortes Conde, *Progreso y Declinacion de la Economia Argentina* (Buenos Aires: Fondo de la Cultura Economica, 1998), 15.

the mines. The people of the local indigenous population were small in stature and slight in build, and the underground working conditions were too harsh for them. The life expectancy of an indigenous miner was less than a year, and this led to the rapid decline of the work force.[12] The discovery of an enormous gold seam in Vila Rica incited the Portuguese to embark on hunting expeditions to capture more slaves. Known as *bandeirantes*, these hunters probed deep into the continent to capture and enslave members of indigenous tribes. Soon they discovered the Guarani nation. This large native population was an easy target for the well-armed bandeirantes, and they made off with hundreds of men, women, and children. They ignored the protests from the Jesuits and even raided the missions. Although the religious order complained about the illegal enslavement of the Guarani, the Spanish crown turned a blind eye toward the conflict.

The monarchy had an obligation to ensure the well-being of the local population, but the government decided to act differently in the case of the bandeirantes. One of the reasons for the total disregard of the natives' welfare was that the entire Iberian Peninsula had come under a single throne in 1580 following the untimely death of Sebastian I of Portugal. The two American colonies continued to be managed separately, but much of the Brazilian mining profits accrued to members of the Spanish nobility. They considered it imperative that the Brazilian mining operations remain profitable.

---

12 In addition to intolerable living and working conditions, the Indians succumbed to the diseases and plagues imported by the Europeans. It is estimated that more than 90 percent of the population was disseminated. As the indigenous population died off, the Europeans felt compelled to import African slaves to perform the mining work and manual labor.

The Jesuits continued to press their case until King Philip IV finally allowed the Guarani to bear arms and defend themselves. In 1641, during a battle that lasted eight days at Mbororé, four thousand armed Guarani defeated a force of three thousand bandeirantes and their Tupi allies. This brought the Portuguese expansion to a halt, and for the next century, the Jesuit missions flourished, but they remained a constant source of political tension. Given the growing resentment of the local merchants against the Jesuit plantations and the pressing needs of the Portuguese for more slaves, the religious order was finally expulsed from the region in 1767. This dark episode left an indelible mark on the conscience of many educated creoles, particularly those who had been educated by the Jesuits at the University of Cordoba. The concepts of social equality and the inherent rights of all humans regardless of race was a theme that would repeat throughout the independence movement, and it was in sharp contrast with the complete disregard for the indigenous population during some of the other revolutions in the region—particularly that of Simon Bolivar's struggle in New Granada. Unfortunately, it was an idea that would not be resurrected for almost two centuries.

In conclusion, Argentina was shaped by its geography. Bracketed by the Andes and Brazil, the estuary of the River Plate served as a natural conduit between the mining operations in Potosi and the outside world. The Spanish colony initially grew out of the booming contraband that flowed up and down the River Plate. This gave it three important characteristics. The first was the relationship between Buenos Aires and the provinces. As the only gateway to the heart of the Spanish empire in Argentina, the port of Buenos Aires was one of the most lucrative markets in the world. Without the provinces, Buenos Aires would have been a lonely outpost in the backwater of a vast empire. Without Buenos Aires, the provinces would have been forced to pay ridiculous fees for goods transported through official channels. Yet, the balance of power between the two would always define the nation's political atmosphere. The second characteristic was the importance of the River Plate. It connected the colony through a network of navigable rivers on which goods, bullion, and information flowed. The third characteristic was the cosmopolitan nature of Buenos Aires. As a major port and marketplace, it attracted a kaleidoscope of nationalities and cultures that created an interesting mix of racial diversity, which was in contrast to most of the other Latin American capitals. The enormous wealth produced by legal and illegal trade also allowed the construction of important universities that raised the level of education and opened the population to innovative ideas.

Revolutionary Fires

The Viceroyalty of the River Plate may have been established in 1776, but it was relatively short-lived. Within a few years, the ideas of the Enlightenment were spurring desires for new forms of government, and an air of revolution was rampant in the Western world. In the same year that the viceroyalty was founded in Argentina, British subjects in North America declared their independence. Four years later, the *comuneros* staged a general uprising in New Granada to protest the egregious government taxes on alcohol and tobacco. In 1789, a dentist, known as Tiradentes, started a rebellion in the Brazilian mining town of Vila Rica to protest unfair taxation and the lack of self-determination. The spirit of liberty was clearly stewing. There was a quest for greater representation and government accountability, and many were rejecting the superstitions of the church and the intolerance of absolutism. The writings of Voltaire and Rousseau espoused equality, freedom, and respect, which encouraged many people to act for themselves, thus stoking the embers of revolution.

At the same time, Spain was experiencing a period of decline. Despite the shiploads of bullion that arrived from the American colonies, the Spanish economy was struggling from centuries of mismanagement. It was not so much that the government was incompetent. The inflow of bullion provided the wrong economic incentives.[13] First, there was no reason for the implementation of fiscal reforms. Tax avoidance was ignored by the monarchy, and government expenses were kept high. Second, there were strong incentives against trade and manufacturing. Most of the trade initiatives were focused on preserving the monopoly rents generated by the colonies. France, England, and Germany took steps to develop domestic industries in textiles and furniture, but Spain saw no need to follow the same path. It relied more heavily on imports than exports to satisfy its demand for manufactured goods. This increased its dependence on external products and led to a steady drain on financial reserves.

There was also an important shift in the ruling composition of the Spanish monarchy at the start of the sixteenth century. The alliance between Castile and Aragon was brief due to the death of Isabela in 1504. Although her husband ruled for a short period after her death, the throne was eventually passed to Charles I, Isabela's grandson. However, Charles's father was the Hapsburg son of the Holy Roman Emperor. This transition of power effectively ceded Spain to the Austrian Hapsburgs, bringing in traditions of endless warfare

---

13 Michael D.Bordo and Roberto Cortés Conde, *Transferring Wealth and Power from the Old to the New World: Monetary and Fiscal Institutions in the 17th through the 19ʰ Centuries* (Cambridge, UK: Cambridge University Press, 2001), 14.

and continental disputes. The Hapsburgs were vehemently opposed to the Reformation—a movement that was transforming the European landscape during the sixteenth century—and because they were emperors of the Holy Roman Empire, their fate was intertwined with the Catholic Church, even though they were often at odds with the pope. The windfall from the Americas not only allowed them to continue their military campaigns, but to expand them even more.

Unfortunately, the income from the colonies was not enough to keep the Spanish economy afloat. As mentioned before, the first shipments of treasure that arrived from the colonies was loot that been stolen from the indigenous population. There had been no cost of extraction. Hence, it was pure profit. This is why remittances from the colonies peaked in 1560, representing a third of all government revenues. The problem was that the funds were not enough to pay for the Hapsburgs' costly military adventures. They were fighting France and the Ottoman Empire, and they were involved in several small skirmishes throughout the continent. The middle of the sixteenth century was the peak of Spanish power, but Charles I left the kingdom saddled with a debt of thirty-six million ducats and an annual deficit of a million ducats. Unable to countenance such obligations, his son, Philip II, defaulted in 1557, his first year on the throne. Nevertheless, he continued to pursue expensive campaigns, including a failed attempt to invade England in 1588 with the Spanish Armada. That naval foray cost him dearly, and he defaulted again in 1596.

One of the reasons costs were spiraling out of control in the colonies was that the Spaniards had very little knowledge of mining, smelting, and metalworking. Their operations were inefficient and expensive. At the same time, the colonists had to build an impressive logistical network to supply the mines, which were a great distance inland. In New Spain and Upper Peru, colonial officials built a series of roads and garrisons to connect the mining communities with the coast. The distances were vast. The trajectory between Lima and Potosi was more than two thousand kilometers, and the colonial administrators needed to provide lodging and security for traveling officials and merchants. The increase in expenses depressed net revenues despite a sharp increase in mining output.[14] Colonial remittances fell to 20 percent of government revenues by the end of the sixteenth century. Already highly dependent on colonial income and struggling under a mountain of debt, the health of the Spanish economy deteriorated. The kingdom was forced to levy extraordinary taxes, which squeezed fiscal policy and pushed the country into a prolonged period of decay.[15] The economic malaise was accompanied by political instability, and a sequence of weak kings allowed themselves to be manipulated by queens, consorts, and high-ranking officials.

The situation came to a head in 1700 with the death of the last Spanish Hapsburg, Charles II. Years of inbreeding had enfeebled the bloodline, and the king was physically infirm and mentally unstable. He died a widower at age thirty-eight and left no successor, and the country plunged into chaos. The throne should have passed to Louis of France, the eld-

---

14 Michael D.Bordo and Roberto Cortés Conde, *Transferring Wealth and Power from the Old to the New World: Monetary and Fiscal Institutions in the 17th through the 19ᵗʰ Centuries* (Cambridge, UK: Cambridge University Press, 2001), 379.

15 Michael D.Bordo and Roberto Cortés Conde, *Transferring Wealth and Power from the Old to the New World: Monetary and Fiscal Institutions in the 17th through the 19ᵗʰ Centuries* (Cambridge, UK: Cambridge University Press, 2001), 147.

est son of Louis XIV, who was married to Charles II's elder half sister. This would have unified the two kingdoms under a single Bourbon monarch, but there was enormous resistance within Europe and the rest of the Hapsburg dynasty. A union between France and Spain would have destabilized the continent's balance of power. Therefore, the two countries came to blows in 1701, and the conflict soon spread far afield. The War of the Spanish Succession ended in 1713 with the Treaty of Utrecht. Although a Bourbon king was finally allowed to gain control of the Spanish throne, it left France with a deep-seated resentment against its western neighbor.

The events of the seventeenth century may seem to be a little confusing, but they help set the stage for the inherent instability that confronted the Spanish colonies. During the rest of the eighteenth century, Spain was ruled by another string of weak monarchs, which accelerated the process of imperial decay. To begin with, the Bourbons were never fully accepted by the Spanish nobility because they were French. Furthermore, the new monarchs tried to implement reforms in order to improve the country's finances. For example, one of the big initiatives was to reduce the operating costs of the colonies. Mining remittances continued to decline as the colonial officials skimmed funds to pay ever-increasing operating costs. As government bureaucracies grew larger, administrative costs rose. There were also ongoing expenses from suppressing indigenous uprisings and pirate attacks.[16] These reforms were what led the crown to convert Buenos Aires into a viceroyalty.

---

16 Michael D.Bordo and Roberto Cortés Conde, *Transferring Wealth and Power from the Old to the New World: Monetary and Fiscal Institutions in the 17th through the 19*[th] *Centuries* (Cambridge, UK: Cambridge University Press, 2001), 13.

At the same time, Spain faced serious problems at its doorstep. By the latter half of the eighteenth century, France had transformed itself from the cradle of the Enlightenment into a furnace of revolution. The Enlightenment unleashed new expressions of government, liberty, and self-determination, all of which flowered into great works of literature, art, and science, but it also sowed the seeds of subversion. Unfortunately, a weakening of the French economy at the end of the eighteenth century provided the spark that led to revolution. The country's military assistance to the North American War of Independence proved to be financially disastrous, and it resulted in a deep recession. The unrest that was produced by the economic downturn exploded into an open revolt against the monarchy in 1792, and the House of Bourbon was dethroned in a hail of musket fire. Out of the ashes of the French Revolution emerged a new form of government. Yet, as is often the case with idealistic movements, the revolution was hijacked by personal ambitions. Purporting to expand the principles of liberty and fraternity, an upstart artillery officer named Napoleon Bonaparte took Paris by storm in 1803, and then he unleashed his revolution on the rest of the continent. This threw the world into disarray, particularly the Spanish colonies. Wealthy creoles were petrified of the implications of such a revolt. The notion of equality and fraternity for all people regardless of class or wealth undermined the institutional structure of the colonial economy and the political structure as well.

The conflict also left Britain in a pinch. It had already gone through a period of bloody civil wars during the middle of the seventeenth century, and it was in no mood to go through the process again. Therefore, it joined the European alliance to suppress Napoleon. One of the measures the British took was to enact a blockade of the major French ports. Napoleon responded by forbidding any of the countries under his domain from trading with British entities. The embargo ultimately culminated into the Continental System, which was designed to inflict pain through economic warfare. As an open trading economy, the island nation found itself in desperate need of new markets. At the same time, Britannia ruled the waves. Under the command of Admiral Lord Nelson, the British navy sank a large part of the French and Spanish fleets during the Battle of Trafalgar in 1805. Nelson's squadron of thirty-three British warships took on a superior force and sank or captured twenty-two enemy vessels without a single loss. This left the British navy unopposed and with the ability to roam freely. Therefore, it was not surprising that the first order of business was to prey on the richest colonies of the Spanish Empire—with Buenos Aires as one of the primary targets.

The British invasion of 1806 was led by General William Beresford. It consisted of sixteen hundred soldiers and a flotilla of twelve warships and transports. Most of the Spanish militia was deployed to the interior parts of the colony to provide defense against the local indigenous tribes. Hence, the port was not prepared to repel the invading force. The British soldiers landed in Quilmes and successfully took the city without much resistance. Given the international nature of the population, many people were initially pleased by the invasion. Most local officials swore allegiance to the British crown, and the city fell under their control. The Spanish viceroy, Marquis Rafael de Sobremonte, tried to flee with the royal treasury to the military garrison in Cordoba, but he was captured in Lujan by a squad of soldiers. He was caught along with more than 1.2 million pesos—equivalent to $25 million today.

A few weeks later, a group of royalists regrouped in the city of Montevideo and counterattacked. The uprising was led by a Frenchman named Santiago de Liniers and a contingent of four thousand creoles. The British soldiers took refuge in the city's main fort, where today sits the Casa Rosada, and they were held under siege for forty days. In a final confrontation that resulted in three hundred casualties, de Liniers routed the British troops. Unfortunately, the treasury had already been sent back to London, and it was never recovered.

The following year, the British returned with a much larger fleet and eight times the number of soldiers. Realizing that the creoles were highly motivated and that the colony was very prosperous, the invading force was better prepared. Under the command of Lieutenant General John Whitelocke, the landing party established a beachhead and disembarked the invasion force. However, de Liniers was also better prepared. After a tactical retreat on the outskirts of the city, the invading force was lured into the center of Buenos Aires. Platoons of militiamen attacked the soldiers in the narrow corridors of the city. Women and servants took to the rooftops and poured scalding water, rocks, and burning debris on the invaders. Sharpshooters and snipers took positions across the city and harassed the thirteen columns of soldiers as they tried to advance. Some of the British finally took refuge in the Convent of Santo Domingo. The militia then surrounded the convent and bombarded it with artillery, resulting in heavy casualties. Whitelocke finally surrendered after losing more than fifteen hundred men.

The two invasions left an indelible mark on the psyche of the creoles. It was clear that with the monarchy in disarray and much of the Spanish fleet at the bottom of the ocean, the colonists would have to fend for themselves. It was also evident that the creoles were competent enough to take on the most formidable navy in the world and defeat it in open battle. This boosted the creoles' self-confidence to such an extent that they felt empowered to demand more of a say over local policies and trade. They would soon have their chance as the situation in Europe deteriorated.

Portugal, which had a long trading relationship with Britain, refused to join Napoleon's continental system. Therefore, the French emperor decided to invade. Lacking a proper navy to take his troops across the Bay of Biscay or through the Straits of Gibraltar, Napoleon had to get his forces across Spanish territory in order to launch his invasion. Spanish Prime Minister Manuel De Godoy acceded to the French request, which resulted in a stealth invasion of his own country. Although the Portuguese monarchy escaped to Brazil onboard a squadron of British naval vessels, Napoleon decided to take control of the entire Iberian Peninsula. It had been a century since the War of Spanish Succession, but there was still a lot of resentment in France because the two thrones had not come together. Napoleon dismissed Charles IV in 1808 and gave him a lifetime pension so that he could live cloistered in a distant castle. Napoleon then installed his carousing brother, Joseph Bonaparte, as king. The events in Spain were disturbing, and the colonists were deeply ashamed. Not only was their king deposed; he had been replaced by Napoleon's drunken brother, commonly known as Pepe Botella.

On a legal basis, the imposition of a new king was binding for the colonists. However, there were several practical reasons why the Spanish creoles did not want to come under French control. The first was economic. Since the Battle of Trafalgar in 1805, the colonists had been free to trade with whomever they wanted. While the merchants in Buenos Aires wanted to obtain their wares at the cheapest prices, they did not want to change their trading arrangement with the miners of Potosi. Over the previous five years, Buenos Aires had enjoyed a huge windfall in profits as its merchants obtained cheaper goods while keeping their prices the same. The second reason that the Spanish creoles did not want the French to gain control of the colonies was political. The defeat of the Canadians during the French and Indian War, also known as the Seven Years War, led to the forced deportation of thousands of Frenchmen. Many were forced to return to France, but the poorer ones were relocated to the other French colonies in the Americas, particularly the swamps and bayous of Louisiana. It was clear that the creoles did not want to suffer a similar fate, particularly if a large group of French colonists was yearning for prosperity. This had already happened in places such as Pernambuco and other parts of the Caribbean when European governments had traded colonies as if they were game pieces on a chessboard.

The creoles were not the only ones who were displeased with the situation. The Spanish were also upset, and a grassroots rebellion soon broke out across the Iberian Peninsula. Various regions banded together to take up arms against the invaders. The groups were known as juntas. The Junta of Cadiz was the strongest of the organizations, but the Junta of Seville was allowed to retain responsibility over the colonies since it was the traditional center of administration for local affairs. Unfortunately, this led to a new set of problems. The British offered the juntas military aid against Napoleon, but in return, they demanded that the American colonies open their ports. The Junta of Seville agreed in 1809. As a result, the colonial resentment against Spanish authority grew even more. Why were they being forced to open their doors to the same country that had recently tried to invade it?

During the next year, the Spanish struggle gained traction, and the French suffered an ignominious defeat at Bailen. However, the incident convinced Napoleon to change tactics. Instead of using small-armed deployments to confront the Spanish guerillas, Napoleon deployed his Grand Armee across the Pyrenees to defeat the uprising and squelch it permanently. With a force of three hundred thousand men, Napoleon descended on Madrid with vengeance as his goal. Faced with overwhelming odds, the juntas collapsed and amalgamated into a single provisional government that took refuge in Cadiz at the end of January 1810. Cut off from the rest of the world, it was clear that the colonies had to rely on themselves and no one else. By May, panic was spreading like wildfire. One by one, the Latin American viceroyalties and captaincies declared their independence. The idea was to set up colonial juntas to continue the struggle against Napoleon. This is why the new governments swore allegiance to the Spanish monarch as they broke away. The creoles invited the members of the viceroyalty to join them in forming a permanent government. They desperately sensed the need to break away before an invading force loomed on the horizon.

Finally, on May 25, 1810, the leading citizens of Buenos Aires broke that city's allegiance to Spain and declared independence. The new government was supposed to be temporary, but no one thought that the Spanish would ever regain their throne. Napoleon seemed to be invincible. Therefore, the notion of allegiance to the crown was rather deceptive. Unfortunately, the French dictator's interests were elsewhere. With his fleet in tatters, he had no way to control his transatlantic possessions. Even before the disaster at Trafalgar, Napoleon negotiated the sale of 2.1 million square kilometers in Louisiana to the United States for 78 million francs. Therefore, he never had imperial ambitions outside of Europe. His focus was farther east. In 1812, Napoleon pulled his army out of Spain to prepare his invasion of Russia. Meanwhile, back in the Americas, the creoles were enjoying the fruits of independence. For some, freedom from European rule meant the ability to pursue individual liberties and self-determination. It meant the end of slavery and the subjugation of the castes. For others, it meant the replacement of the European overlords with themselves as the new masters. This group had no interest in changing the status quo other than the appropriation of the monopoly rents. Hence, there were two opposing views of what independence meant.

The two groups quickly polarized into divergent sides with the more conservative members vehemently opposed to liberal principles. This type of division occurred throughout the colonies, particularly in New Granada and Chile. Many of the native-born Spaniards sided with the more conservative members of society, which included the clergy, former government officials, and merchants. Intellectuals, military officers, and members of the lower caste took up the liberal cause. Although the former group had a great deal of wealth, the latter was larger in number. This schism would repeatedly draw political lines throughout the region in ensuing years.

Among the more liberal elements of the new government was a group of young intellectuals that included Mariano Moreno, Juan José Castelli, and Manuel Belgrano. The three men strongly believed in the principles of the Enlightenment. Fearing a counterrevolution, the colonial junta dispatched a military force to arrest Spanish officials and execute them, including Santiago de Liniers. Although he repelled the British invasions, de Liniers was perceived to have strong connections to France due to his lineage and birth. He had also been appointed viceroy in 1807. The execution of such a prominent person sparked panic among many residents, and some immediately decamped for the colonies that were still under European control. Other royalists escaped to the other side of the River Plate to build a reactionary force against the revolutionaries. The bulk of the royalist forces, which were located farther upriver, led a campaign of harassment that kept the Northern provinces in a constant state of war. In the meantime, the junta in Buenos Aires continued to polarize. The concepts proposed by the liberals, particularly the emancipation of slaves and universal suffrage, were too much for the more conservative factions to accept.

Although the conservatives were outnumbered, their wealth soon allowed them to gain the upper hand. Led by Cornelio Saavedra, a creole of high birth, they began to dominate the political agenda. Eager to fight for the cause, they dispatched the young idealists on various suicide missions. Castelli was sent to combat the royalists in Upper Peru. Belgrano was dispatched to Paraguay, and Moreno was sent to London to gather international support. Unfortunately, he was poisoned, and died en route. The military expeditions were not just an attempt to be rid of the more radical elements of the junta; the lifeblood of Buenos Aires depended on the North's independence from Spain. Without the trade that flowed upriver, the port of Buenos Aires would be a solitary garrison on the banks of a godforsaken territory. With the mines of Potosi still in Spanish hands, Buenos Aires and the Northern provinces found themselves with opposing interests. The Northern provinces did not want to do anything that would spoil their commercial relationship with the miners. Therefore, Buenos Aires needed to liberate the region so that it could be free to trade.

For two years, the valiant Belgrano fought the royalists in Upper Peru with thin supplies and a small number of men, most of whom had almost no military training. The valiant liberal was blindly committed to the cause, and he roused his ill-equipped troops with stirring speeches and symbols. He even designed the country's flag. However, in 1813, after a rousing defeat at the Battle of Ayahuma, the junta decided to relieve Belgrano with General José de San Martin. The young general was a veteran of the peninsular wars against the French. He was a native of the Province of Corrientes, where he was born in the town of Yapeyu in 1778. San Martin's father was one of the Spanish administrators who were sent to manage the missions after the Jesuits were expelled. The cruelty imparted on the indigenous tribes left an indelible mark on the young man. His family returned to Spain in 1783, where he joined the army. San Martin made a name for himself, and eventually he earned the rank of lieutenant colonel. He fought with distinction at the victorious Battles of Arjonilla and Bailen. Many creoles joined the Spanish militias in the fight against Napoleon. However, there was a sinking realization that they would never be fully accepted after the war. Therefore, the best option was to return home. As the war was winding down in 1812, San Martin decided to leave for Buenos Aires. Initially, the residents of the city distrusted the dashing young officer because they thought he was a royal spy. However, when he married a local aristocrat's daughter, he was gradually accepted into society.

The young officer was then dispatched to relieve Belgrano and to lead the army of the North. His arrival was met with quick results, and he was able to stabilize the Northern frontier. However, San Martin had a new problem to confront. Napoleon's move into Russia allowed the Spanish to regain control of their government, and Ferdinand VII was restored to the throne. Although the French occupation devastated the country, it also imbued it with an air of liberalism. Ferdinand VII was allowed to return, but he was no longer treated as an absolute monarch. The Spanish Constitution of 1812 established a new organizational framework that permitted universal suffrage and expanded the power of the legislative assembly. Despite the rhetoric about liberty and freedom, the creoles knew that it was only a matter of time until the Spanish returned to reclaim their precious territories. Fear ran high throughout the land. Most of the creoles had sworn loyalty to the king, but they were in no mood to give up their newfound economic and political liberties. Great fortunes had been amassed since the departure of the royalists, and the creoles enjoyed governing their own affairs.

In February 1815, the colonies' worst fears were realized when Spanish troops began disembarking in New Granada and Peru. At first, the process was gradual. The objective of the invasion force was to regain control of the principal mining regions. However, with the final defeat of Napoleon at Waterloo in June 1815, the Spanish knew that they could safely direct all of their military resources into reconquering the last remaining colonies. In late 1815, the revolutionary government in Chile fell, and the royalist forces in Upper Peru began launching attacks as they pushed into northern Argentina. The former Viceroyalty of the River Plate was the last bastion of independence, and it was now under serious threat. With Chile under Spanish control, the royalists could launch an invasion across the Andes at any time and take Buenos Aires by complete surprise. The city leaders knew that the royal sympathizers inside the colony would willingly assist an invading force. Therefore, Buenos Aires decided to counter with its own invasion of Chile to defeat the Spanish royalists.

In July 1816, San Martin was dispatched to Cuyo to assemble an invasion force. Cuyo sits just across the Andes from the Chilean capital of Santiago. In order to guard his northern flank, he appointed Miguel de Guemes to interdict the royalist attacks that were being launched from Upper Peru. For the next six months, San Martin worked on the preparations for the perilous crossing. He amassed a force of ten thousand mules, four thousand head of cattle, forty tons of food, and fifty-two hundred men. He set up munitions factories to make firearms and gunpowder, and he established foundries to produce cannons and cannonballs. The creole government knew that the Spanish were still reeling from the French invasion, but Buenos Aires needed to secure foreign assistance if they were to expel the royalists from the continent. This would require a formal declaration of independence from the

Spanish monarch, but first they needed to resolve their own differences.

As San Martin was making his invasion preparations, a national congress was convened in the northern city of Tucuman. The reason it was held in the chilly foothills of the Andes, and not in the bustling metropolis of Buenos Aires, was to stress the overall importance of the provincial region. However, this was nothing more than a symbolic gesture. Most of the power was still in the hands of Buenos Aires. The assignment of delegates was based on population, thus giving the city an overwhelming presence at the convention. On July 9, 1816, after a great deal of debate on institutional design, the delegates finally declared full independence from Spain.[17] Now, the hard part was to come.

In late January 1817, San Martin set out for the Andes, a journey that entailed crossing five hundred kilometers of rugged terrain and scaling almost three thousand meters over sea level. Unfortunately, the royalists were waiting on the other side. In a series of fiery confrontations, San Martin routed the Spanish and secured the independence of Chile. Yet, there was still a threat emanating from Upper Peru. In order to remove the attacks on the Northern provinces, he needed to carry out the remaining components of the Maitland Plan and invade Lima. This would remove the main source of support for the Spanish forces that were deployed in the altiplano, thus allowing his troops to neutralize the northern front. The preparations for the invasion were complex because they needed a fleet. Fortunately, San Martin secured the services of Thomas Cochrane, a British naval mercenary. Interestingly,

---

17 In order to stress the notion that the new republic was a confederation of unified states, the first name of the nation was The United Provinces of the River Plate.

Buenos Aires was not so convinced of the need to expend additional resources on defeating the royalists in Peru. Nevertheless, in 1820, San Martin gathered the funds, men, and ships needed to launch his invasion force. Using a flotilla of eight warships and eleven gunboats, he disembarked his forces in Lima and laid siege to the city, eventually routing the royalist garrison. The viceroy and his troops escaped into the sierra, and in 1821, San Martin became Peru's liberator and first president. By this time, he had lost all support from Buenos Aires. His objective of eliminating the Spanish threat from his country's borders was also completed. Therefore, San Martin decided to return to Buenos Aires in 1822 after a conference with Simon Bolivar in Guayaquil.

Argentina's independence was born out of an existential need for survival against the menace of foreign invasion. The creole way of life was threatened by the spirit of a revolution that promised to alter the social and economic system that had been in place since the birth of the colony. There was also a need to prevent the forced expulsion that had been experienced in some of the other colonies that had changed hands. However, the process of independence unleashed political forces that were simmering below the surface. One element wanted to preserve the status quo, and the other element wanted to remedy the social inequalities that had repressed a large part of the population for a long time.

The embers of the revolutionary fires still burn brightly in Argentina today, and they help to define the schism between the political left and right.

The Struggle for Supremacy

The war against Spain continued for another dozen years, but the independence of Chile and Peru removed the imminent threat of invasion, thus allowing the government to refocus on internal affairs. The ideological differences between the conservative and liberal factions gave way to more pressing economic issues, such as the balance of power between Buenos Aires and the provinces. The colonial period established the symbiotic relationship between them. Buenos Aires could not exist without the markets and products provided by the provinces. At the same time, the provinces needed Buenos Aires as their gateway to the world. As much as the young intellectuals of the revolution were attracted to the enlightened principles of liberty and fraternity, they needed to preserve the commercial relationship with the more conservative factions in the interior to keep the economy afloat. The Argentine struggle between the center and the periphery was embodied in the competition between Juan Manuel de Rosas and Justo José de Urquiza. These two strongmen personified the *caudillo*—the political figure that emerged from the collapse of the Spanish imperial system. There were scores of caudillos throughout the territory, but these two were the most powerful. Both were extremely wealthy members of the landed aristocracy. They defended their interests and used their provinces as personal fiefdoms. They also showed that the only way that anyone could assert control over the country was by physically taking over Buenos Aires.

The conflict between the center of the country and the periphery initially took the form of confrontation between the Unitarian and Federalist parties. Both sides argued that their form of government represented continuity with colonial traditions. The Unitarians advocated a centralist organization with all power and decision-making based in Buenos Aires. This was in line with the monarchy's absolutist practices and its focus on preserving social order. The Federalists pushed for a decentralized form of government that gave the provinces autonomy in making policy decisions. Under the Spanish regime, the provinces enjoyed a great deal of independence, considering the enormous distances involved. They collected local taxes and implemented laws. The Federalists argued that a reversion to a Unitarian form of government would be a move in the opposite direction. The provinces would surrender much of the freedom they enjoyed as members of the empire.

At first, the differences between the two sides were settled in debates, but things became tenuous as time wore on. By 1820, as San Martin was preparing to invade Peru, the Unitarians and the Federalists came to blows at the Battle of Cepeda on the border of Buenos Aires and Santa Fe. Greatly outnumbered by an army led by provincial caudillos, Buenos

Aires recalled the various armies that were fighting on the frontier. However, San Martin refused to abandon the field for fear that the Spanish would invade. He also rebuffed the notion of using the national army to settle internal political disputes. Therefore, the Unitarians were soundly defeated. At the heart of the dispute was the issue of money. Buenos Aires had convinced the provinces to join its independence movement, but it refused to share its tariff revenues. Its unwillingness to redistribute these resources caused the country to be unable to consolidate itself under a monopoly of legitimate authority for more than four decades.

The Argentine economy was also undergoing profound changes at the turn of the eighteenth century. By the start of the War of Independence, the mines of Potosi were in an advanced state of decline. Maintenance had been reduced by the necessities of the conflict, and many mineshafts had flooded. As a result, the booming industry and trade that drove the Northern provinces was weakened. At the same time, a new source of economic activity was developing farther south. Landowners began using the verdant pastures of the pampas to herd cattle in order to produce leather, hides, and salted meat for export. From a macroeconomic standpoint, the decline in silver production was netted out by the rise in agricultural exports. This meant that the tariffs collected by the customs house remained steady. However, the changes in the location of economic activity had important implications for the regional distribution of power. As the locus of activity shifted downriver, the clout of Buenos Aires grew even more powerful.[18]

---

18 Roberto Cortes Conde, *Progreso y Declinacion de la Economia Argentina* (Buenos Aires: Fondo de la Cultura Economica, 1998), 13.

Merchants increased their landholdings in the grasslands outside of Buenos Aires, but they faced new challenges in managing their ranching operations. The power vacuum created by the collapse of the colonial system allowed the proliferation of marauding bands of gauchos and brigands to do as they saw fit. They stole cattle and attacked farms. The inability of the provinces to agree on a common form of government produced a general sense of anarchy, and this threatened the newly established agrarian economy. Therefore, the landowners banded together to pacify the countryside. One of the largest landowners in Buenos Aires was Juan Manuel de Rosas. Rich and ruthless, he restored law and order on the pampas and emerged as the region's leading political figure. At the same time, the country was under the threat of being carved apart by armed raiders from Brazil. The eastern shore of the River Plate, today known as Uruguay, was invaded by Portuguese imperial forces. Provincial leaders realized that they needed to unify in order to avert foreign invasion. However, they first needed to agree on a national political framework. In 1826, provincial delegates, with a large component from Buenos Aires, met to draft a constitution. The country's name was changed to Argentina, and the appellation The United Provinces of the River Plate was dropped. The constitutional assembly drafted articles of incorporation that created a strong centralized government, and they appointed Bernardino Rivadavia as the country's first chief executive.

Rivadavia was a professional bureaucrat, having served as a diplomat and government minister. During an official mission to England, he became enamored with the advances of the Industrial Revolution. As President of Argentina, he founded museums and the University of Buenos Aires. He also took out the country's first foreign loan, from Baring Brothers, and promised to build public works and to establish forts to repel Indian attacks. Unfortunately, none of this was done, and most of the funds disappeared under mysterious circumstances. Within two years, the loan was in default, and it brought the city of London to its knees. Yet, Rivadavia played an important role in Argentine history, despite being the country's first president and leader to default on a foreign obligation. The unification of the country under his leadership neutered the Brazilian threat. Argentine forces invaded Uruguay and defeated the Portuguese in a series of land and naval engagements. Yet, once the threat of invasion subsided, the provinces' support for Rivadavia evaporated. He was a Unitarian construct, and the Federalist cause still burned strongly in the hinterland. Hence, the Constitution of 1826 was never ratified, and Rivadavia served only one year in office.

Rivadavia's departure in 1827 led to another period of political instability. One of the interesting characteristics of Latin America society is its tendency to descend into anarchy. This weakness was capitalized upon by future President Domingo Faustino Sarmiento. He argued that the ruggedness of the geography produced the continent's penchant for savagery. However, a better explanation could be the rigidness of the social structure. Given the caste system that was embedded since the founding of the colonies, a centralized enforcement agency was the only thing that restrained the underclasses from rebelling. Hence, a collapse of government authority would lead to a breakdown of social order. In any case, the fear of anarchy is a common thread across the

Latin American body politic. The words *Order and Progress* are emblazoned on the Brazilian Flag. Colombia's national motto is *Order and Liberty*. This gives a conservative and authoritarian bent to Latin American politics, and it produces a general distrust of democracy. Indeed, if the Argentine military perceived governments as being too democratic, it would topple them for fear that such a movement would lead to mob rule and chaos. That is why the departure of Rivadavia saw the emergence of Juan Manuel de Rosas as the governor of Buenos Aires. There was a need to have a strong figure to restore order and to defend the city's interests.

For the next twenty years, Rosas formally or informally ruled Argentina. His style was authoritarian and confrontational, and he used special powers to rule by decree—an approach that he used repeatedly. He also employed a militant arm, the Mazorca, which ruthlessly enforced many of his edicts and ensured loyalty. Rosas's objective was the expansion of Buenos Aires's power, and he achieved it by pushing the country's frontier deeper into the south and west. In order to consolidate the city's dominant position, he prohibited the free navigation of the Parana and Paraguay Rivers, thus keeping Buenos Aires as the sole port of embarkation for all trade. This assured that all tariff duties would continue to pass through the city's customs house. To highlight the importance of the customs house, it generated 80 to 90 percent of the country's public sector revenues.[19]

Rosas also allowed Uruguay to split away and become a sovereign nation. One of the mysteries of Argentine history is why it allowed Uruguay to secede after the Portuguese forces

---

19 Aldo Ferrer, La Economía Argentina: Desde sus Orígenes hasta los Principios del Siglo XXI (Buenos Aires: Fondo de Cultura Económica, 2004), 141.

were defeated. It is often said that Uruguay was created to establish a buffer state between Argentina and Brazil. The British wanted to ensure that the River Plate would be treated as an international waterway, given that it would mark the boundary between two sovereign states. Under international law, such a boundary ensured free navigation for foreign vessels. Otherwise, the River Plate would have been fully under Argentine sovereignty and closed to international traffic. Brazil was also interested in ensuring fluvial access to its southwestern states of Rio Grande do Sul, Santa Catarina, Parana, and Mato Grosso. Nevertheless, the willingness of Buenos Aires to surrender an important part of its territory, with huge grazing pastures and resources, was probably driven by a hidden or overt desire to rid itself of an important rival.

Montevideo is a much better port than Buenos Aires. It is deep water and sits on the Atlantic, which was an important consideration as cargo ships became bigger and with deeper drafts. Buenos Aires was initially established as a center of contraband and later as a tollbooth for vessels that were making their way up the network of rivers. Now, however, it transformed itself into a major shipping and warehousing center. It required constant dredging and the construction of special port facilities. Therefore, it was only a matter of time until Montevideo displaced Buenos Aires as the natural point of entry. However, this could be averted by allowing Uruguay to split away. That would leave Buenos Aires as the only natural point of entry into Argentina. If this theory were true, it would highlight the lengths to which Rosas would go to ensure the supremacy of Buenos Aires over the rest of the county.

Rosas's monopolization of trade through Buenos Aires did not engender many friends abroad or at home. In 1845,

France and Britain dispatched a squadron of warships to blockade the port and force the truculent Rosas to allow the free navigation of the rivers. Both countries wanted to tap the rich trade opportunities provided by the provinces. Despite a valiant attempt by the Argentine military to thwart the blockade, the squadron effectively shut down the port, but their effort was to no avail. The costs of maintaining the blockade were greater than the economic benefits, and the blockade was lifted. Regardless, Rosas soon discovered that he faced powerful opponents in his own backyard.

In 1851, Urquiza had enough of Rosas, and he devised a plan to thwart him. He had been a close ally of Rosas's, but he had grown tired of his tyrannical policies. While Rosas dominated the rich pastures outside Buenos Aires, Urquizas's domain was Entre Rios—the river delta bracketed by the Parana and Uruguay Rivers. The region is very rich in farming and cattle ranching and has several deepwater ports along the Parana River. Urquiza built up a large fortune in agriculture, finance, and transportation. He also knew that his province would be even more prosperous if foreign cargo ships were allowed to dock directly at his ports. Therefore, he joined forces with Corrientes (another riverine province), Brazil, and scores of exiled Argentines to take on Buenos Aires.

The participation of Brazil was due to a new foreign policy position that Rosas was espousing. Even though he had allowed Uruguay to split away, he had developed a change of heart. He expounded at length about how he planned to recapture it, as well as Paraguay, in order to recreate the Viceroyalty of the River Plate. This would have been a terrible blow for Brazil, as that country would have lost riverine access to its southwestern states. Therefore, the Brazilians decided to join forces with Urquiza. They contributed most of the funds, ships, and half of the troops that were used in the campaign.

The Argentine general assembled his coalition and met Rosas at the town of Caseros on the outskirts of Buenos Aires on February 3, 1852. Rosas's forces were no match for the huge alliance, and they were easily routed. As a result, he was forced to flee the field of battle and Argentina. In the end, the despot was politically isolated. He alienated many of his followers, and most of his troops failed to fight. This very scenario would be repeated almost a century later when Juan Domingo Peron, another powerful and despotic leader, would be trounced. Rosas's sudden departure created a vacuum that pushed the city into chaos, and there was mass looting by the victorious troops.[20]

Urquiza quickly moved to establish a new decentralized government. He shut down the customs house in Buenos Aires, thus permitting the free navigation of the rivers, and he allowed each provincial government to collect its own tariffs. Yet, instead of occupying the city and converting it into his bastion of power, Urquiza returned to Entre Rios to manage his own personal affairs. He left a small military garrison inside Buenos Aires, but the city was on its own. This turned out to be a strategic mistake. Although defeated, Buenos Aires was still rich and powerful, and there was a great deal of resentment against Urquiza. Most of the prisoners of war who were captured at Caseros were executed, and Urquiza did nothing to detain the sacking of the city. Therefore, the leading citizens and merchants armed themselves and took to the field of battle once more. This time it was without Rosas. Nevertheless,

---

20 William Jeffrey, *Mitre and Argentina* (New York: Library Publisher, 1952), 65-69.

the outcome was the same, and Buenos Aires was forced to sign the Treaty of San Nicolas, whereby it named Urquiza the head of the confederation. The terms of the treaty included the creation of a new constitutional congress. However, the representatives from Buenos Aires refused to participate. They knew that the new constitution would strip them of the power to control trade and collect customs tariffs. Therefore, they decided to secede from the confederation and establish their own sovereign state.

Buenos Aires's decision to leave the confederation was an act of rebellion and a reflection of the transformation that was taking place in the Argentine economy. Under the colonial system, the city was a virtual tollbooth. Therefore, it needed to maintain a good relationship with the provinces. However, with the depletion of the mines, the center of economic activity had moved to the grasslands outside the city and to the pampas of Santa Fe and Entre Rios.[21] Therefore, Buenos Aires could survive on the revenues that were being generated with its own resources, thus freeing it from the shackles of provincial trade.

Not perceiving the changes that were taking place, the provinces continued to work on creating a federalist form of government. In 1852, the constitutional congress convened in Santa Fe to put together a national framework. Drafted by Juan Bautista Alberdi, a renowned legal scholar, the constitution employed many of the basic principles of governance set forth in the United States Constitution, such as the rights of individuals and the division of governmental powers. However, Buenos Aires refused to acknowledge or sign the docu-

---

21 Roberto Cortes Conde, *The First Stages of Modernization in Spanish America* (New York: Harper & Row, 1974), 119.

ment. Relations with the provinces were growing hostile, and Buenos Aires declared an embargo on all riverine trade, thus throttling the provincial economies.[22] While the provinces languished, Buenos Aires grew prosperous. Foreign investment poured in, financing the building of ports, railroads, and telegraph lines. Many of the city's merchants made fortunes by returning to their old business of acting as agents of contraband.

It was at this time that Buenos Aires developed its extensive rail network. The first line was inaugurated in 1857.[23] Not to be outdone, the confederation followed suit with its own railroad that connected the port of Rosario with the city of Cordoba. Urquiza recognized the railroad's benefits in reducing shipping costs, opening up new markets, and facilitating the mobilization of resources. Yet, the provincial economies were still suffering from the embargo. There was a lack of manufactured goods and no way for farmers to export their products. Therefore, Urquiza raised another army in 1859 to take on Buenos Aires. The two forces met once more at the dusty town of Cepeda. This time the troops of Buenos Aires were led by a young officer, Bartolome Mitre, who had fought with distinction against Rosas in Uruguay.

Once more, the provincial forces were victorious, and Urquiza dictated the terms of the peace accord. This became known as the Pact of San José de Flores, but it was nothing more than a new version of the Pact of San Nicolas. This time Buenos Aires was not allowed to opt out of the confederation.

---

22 Roberto Cortes Conde, *Progreso y Declinacion de la Economia Argentina* (Buenos Aires: Fondo de la Cultura Economica, 1998), 15.

23 Juan Manuel Santa Cruz, *Ferrocarriles Argentinos* (Buenos Aires: Facultad de Ciencias Economicas, Comerciales y Politicas, 1966), 12-16.

Urquiza stipulated that it join the other provinces in accepting the Constitution of 1853. He demanded that it forfeit all foreign embassies and diplomatic relations. The customs house was nationalized, and the income was proportionally divided among the provinces. At the same time, the city of Buenos Aires was separated from the province and made into a federal district. The governor of Buenos Aires was ordered to sign the document then resign and call for new elections.

It didn't take long for Buenos Aires to rebel once again. It was too powerful to be humiliated. Therefore, under the leadership of Mitre, they rearmed. They poured money into purchasing modern weapons and obtaining the latest drilling techniques. Ready to fight, Mitre goaded Urquiza back to the field of battle. This time, the two forces met at the town of Pavon on September 17, 1861. Realizing that he faced a superior force, Urquiza suddenly abandoned his army and returned to his home in Entre Rios. Many Federalists considered him a traitor, and he was assassinated years later by one of his closest lieutenants. This was the only time that Buenos Aires was able to face down the provinces, but it still left an important lesson for future Argentine leaders: Buenos Aires could be defeated by a confederation of the provinces, but the only way to take control of the national apparatus was to occupy the city.

Rosas and Urquiza were powerful men who embodied the struggle for supremacy between Buenos Aires and the provinces. They left an indelible mark on the national psyche. Rosas cemented the dominant position of Buenos Aires, but Urquiza coerced it into the confederation. The entity that emerged was the Argentine state. The impasse was resolved by establishing an equilibrium that allowed Buenos Aires to control the nation as long as it shared the proceeds that were generated by the port. This became one of the country's main institutional pillars. Known as coparticipation, it was a fiscal mechanism forged in the crucible of battle. Altering it would always lead to political, economic, and social instability. With the definition of the Argentine state, it was time to move on to the creation of the nation.

The Birth of the Nation

Buenos Aires broke the back of the confederation at the Battle of Pavon, but in many ways, Urquiza won the war. The Pacts of San Nicolas and San José de Flores forced Buenos Aires to coalesce with the provinces. Yet, the unified state was not a nation. A bloody revolution had been fought to preserve a colonial way of life. It was followed by a protracted civil war to determine the relationship between the provinces and the port that served as the gateway to the world. However, the two main sections of the country had little in common. Like a pair of Siamese twins that did not care for each other, each tried to break away. Therefore, Argentina needed to forge itself into a nation with a common sense of identity and a collective purpose. To that end, three leaders played a critical role. Bartolome Mitre, Domingo Faustino Sarmiento, and Julio Argentino Roca used the sword, book, and plough to create the ethereal notion of the Argentine nation, thus converting the territory into a vision of prosperity and development.

Rivadavia was the first president of Argentina, but he was the temporary leader of an organizational framework that was never fully accepted by all of the provinces. Mitre was the first president who was appointed by the unified state operating under a ratified constitution. In 1862, he began his term by trying to forge national unity. To that end, he installed new provincial governors who were loyal to Buenos Aires. Likewise, he fostered a common economic approach by eliminating the provincial currencies. Mitre was extremely pragmatic, but he also was somewhat of an ideologue. In his youth, he was exiled to Chile for his opposition to Rosas. There, he developed a passion for journalism, and often took up lost causes.[24] Later in life, he established the country's newspaper of record, *La Nacion*. He was also a skilled orator, and was able to move large crowds with stirring speeches. Mitre was more in line with the liberals of the revolution who pursued a progressive form of government. He espoused universal education, the modernization of infrastructure, and agrarian reform. However, he strongly believed that such progress could only be achieved under the command of a unified democratic state. The problem was that certain areas of the country were ruled by local caudillos who refused to adhere to the commands of Buenos Aires. The new Argentine president needed to bring them to heel. Fortunately, an opportunity to rally the nation under his command would appear when Argentina was forced to go to war against Paraguay.

Paraguay had been part of the Viceroyalty of the River Plate. Bereft of mineral resources, at least in the form of sil-

---

24 William Jeffrey, *Mitre and Argentina* (New York: Library Publisher, 1952), 58.

ver and gold, it was better known for its large population of Guarani Indians. Hence, it was put under the auspices of the Catholic Church, which set up a system of missions in order to proselytize to the local population and use their labor to produce products for the miners of Potosi. Once the War of Independence started, Paraguay split off and isolated itself into a hermit state. Attempts by Belgrano to reintegrate it with the new federation of provinces failed, and it was mostly forgotten. Buenos Aires was more concerned with eradicating the Spanish threat from its western and northern flanks. After this was accomplished, the provinces turned their attention to resolving their internal disputes, leaving the issue of Paraguay aside. Unfortunately, the country had a major disadvantage. It was landlocked. Brazil was to the north and east, Bolivia to the west, and Argentina to the south. Hence, its only access to the world was through the rivers that drained into the River Plate. That forced Paraguay to have a dependent relationship with Argentina, which was a constant source of political stress.

The strongly hierarchical nature of the Paraguayan colonial system, which allowed a small group of clergymen to govern a large indigenous population, was imbued with a legacy of autocracy. Democratic traditions in Latin America were thin, but they were nonexistent in Paraguay. It was against this backdrop that Paraguay came under the rein of a series of very strong paternalistic leaders, starting with José Gaspar Rodriquez de Francia. He was succeeded by his nephew, Carlos Antonio Lopez, and then his son, Francisco Solano Lopez. Despotic and tyrannical in nature, these leaders also had a modernistic bent. They built the region's first railroad as well as telegraph systems and shipyards for making steel-hulled vessels. They fielded the largest army in South America, equipped it with the latest armament, and brought in European drill instructors to train the soldiers to impeccable standards. The Paraguayan economy was doing well during the middle part of the nineteenth century. It had a vibrant agrarian economy growing yerba mate, tobacco, grains, and timber. However, the national leadership knew that it could become more prosperous if it had direct access to a deepwater port on the Atlantic.

The opportunity for expansion arrived in 1862, when Francisco Solano Lopez rose to the presidency upon his father's death. A bombastic leader with a Napoleonic complex, Solano Lopez found himself at the head of a standing army of forty-four thousand men. Argentina's army had fewer than five thousand soldiers, and most of them were deployed along the frontier to defend the settlements against Indian attacks.[25] Brazil's army was larger, but the troops were also dispersed across the vast territory. Uruguay's armed forces were nonexistent, since the country was broke. Years of civil war left the government's coffers empty. Moreover, Paraguay's infrastructure was perfectly suited for war. The railroad quickly transported troops across the small territory. The foundries smelted the iron and steel needed for armament. The shipyards turned out warships to defend against riverine attacks, and the telegraph system kept the nation's leadership well informed about what was going on at the front. Hence, the high command could deploy troops and equipment in the most efficient manner. Having the ways and means to go to war, Paraguay was looking for the slightest pretense to take on its neighbors.

---

25 William Jeffrey, *Mitre and Argentina* (New York: Library Publisher, 1952), pp. 196-197.

At the same time, Uruguay was in one of its perennial tussles between the two main political factions—the Blancos and Colorados. The presidency was in the hands of Atanasio Aguirre, a Blanco. However, Venancio Flores, a Colorado and close friend of Mitre, launched a coup d'état. The fighting plunged Uruguay into chaos, and the bloodshed spilled into Brazil. In an effort to stabilize its border, Brazilian troops entered Uruguay to restore law and order. This led President Aguirre to plead for help from Paraguay on the pretense that his country was being invaded. The Paraguayan military immediately responded by crossing through Argentina to help its Uruguayan ally, but it was to no avail. Aguirre had already stepped down. Paraguayan President Solano Lopez then retaliated against Brazil by invading Mato Grosso. Solano Lopez's ultimate objective was to drive a wedge through the southern fringe of Brazil and gain access to the Atlantic. He also hoped to arouse the resentment that festered in the northern Argentine provinces in the hope that they would secede and become part of a greater Paraguay. Faced by such blatant aggression, Argentina, Brazil, and Uruguay formed the Triple Alliance in 1865 and named Mitre as head of the coalition.

It was ironic that Mitre was put at the head of the campaign. He was initially against the war. He was more focused on pacifying the wayward bands of gauchos and caudillos that still roamed the provinces. There was also a great deal of domestic resistance to the conflict, particularly in the northern part of Argentina, where people had more kinship with the Paraguayans than with the Brazilians.[26] The Paraguayans were Spanish speakers whose ancestors were

---

26 William Jeffrey, *Mitre and Argentina* (New York: Library Publisher, 1952), 212.

once members of the same viceroyalty. Meanwhile, the Brazilians were Portuguese speakers with a culture that was generally hostile to Spain. Nevertheless, Mitre needed the war to unify the nation. He wanted a crucible of fire to create a common purpose.

Interestingly, this process was being repeated across the globe. The middle part of the eighteenth century marked the rise of the modern nation-state. The Treaty of Westphalia of 1648 recognized that individual sovereignties were independent of dynastic European empires such as the Hapsburgs and Bourbons. Although it took another two hundred years to manifest itself fully, the middle part of the 1800s witnessed an amalgamation process whereby countries with similar cultures merged into monolithic nations. The Italian states came together in the Risorgimento. Bismarck used the conflict with France, through the Franco-Prussian War, to meld his states into a single nation with a common purpose. The United States was using blood and guns to define its national vision and coalesce under a single political, social, and economic format. Across the Andes, Chile was using military means to expand its frontier and secure its future as one of the more prosperous nations of the region. Therefore, the War of the Triple Alliance played well into Mitre's hands. Unwittingly, Solano Lopez provided the Argentine president with the opportunity to forge his country together by pursuing a collective cause through the persecution of a common enemy.

Unfortunately, the war did not begin well for the Triple Alliance. They lacked the manpower, equipment, and training of the Paraguayans. Fortunately, strategic and tactical mistakes by Solano Lopez allowed the alliance to expulse the enemy from Brazil and Argentina by 1865. Yet, the allies were not content with regaining the territory that had been lost. They were intent on invading Paraguay in order to topple Solano Lopez and make the country pay for the cost of the conflict. Restoring the old borders would have put an end to the fighting, but the war was now seen as an opportunity to conquer a weaker state. Unbeknownst to the allies, they were about to face one of the most humiliating losses in military history.

After routing the Paraguayans at the Battle of Tuyuti on May 24, 1866, where thirty-five thousand allied soldiers took on an inferior force of twenty-four thousand Paraguayans, the alliance found itself in very bright spirits. In a parallel operation, the Brazilian navy defeated its Paraguayan counterpart when it sank a large portion of the enemy fleet at the Battle of Riachuelo. A Paraguayan squadron tried to ambush a larger Brazilian detachment in the early morning, but a series of mistakes and bad luck turned the attack into disaster. Therefore, it was not surprising to find the allies with an air of invincibility as they faced the opposition at Curupaiti three months later. A force of five thousand Paraguayans, with fewer than fifty cannons, faced a superior group of twenty thousand allied troops that were supported by the Brazilian navy. The joint operation began with a thunderous naval bombardment that was followed by a resounding infantry charge, with Mitre leading the way. The charge, which was composed solely of Argentine and Uruguayan soldiers, commenced before the naval bombardment ended, thus creating a sense of confusion. Furthermore, the Brazilian navy was targeting the empty trenches in the rear, leaving the bulk of the enemy unscathed. As the oncoming soldiers entered the open field, they were set upon by a Paraguayan artillery barrage. Defending troops that were ensconced in the trenches also opened fire, cutting down almost half of the allied soldiers—including the son of future President Domingo Faustino Sarmiento. More than nine thousand allied men were lost, compared to a loss of fewer than fifty Paraguayans. Yet, Solano Lopez failed to take advantage of his victory when he chose not to pursue the retreating forces as they fled the field.

The defeat at Curupaiti was a terrible setback for the allies. The war was halted for two years while the coalition regrouped and decided what to do. Up to that moment, everyone had thought that the conflict was over. To the contrary, the rout had reignited the doubts that were simmering below the surface. Why was the alliance still fighting Paraguay when its troops were driven out of Brazil, Argentina, and Uruguay? Moreover, why was Argentina fighting against a fellow Spanish-speaking nation? It was clear that a small cadre of Argentine merchants were becoming increasingly rich by providing food and arms for the war effort. A new loan had been taken out from Baring Brothers to pursue the campaign, and great fortunes were being made in Buenos Aires. Even Urquiza, the champion of the Federalist cause, was making a bonanza by providing supplies, meat, and beasts of burden. No wonder he was ignoring the Federalist drumbeat. This is why in the aftermath of Curupaiti, several of the provinces exploded into open rebellion.

Sensing that the war was lost and that Mitre was more worried about problems on the home front, Solano Lopez approached the allied leader and tried to negotiate a peace accord in September 1866. Mitre was initially receptive, but the Brazilians were not. They saw Solano Lopez and Paraguay as too much of a threat. It was not so much that they feared an invasion, but they realized that a powerful military leader in Paraguay could cut off the access that the south-western Brazilian states had to the Parana and Paraguay Rivers. Therefore, they were prepared to continue the war until the country was annihilated. Unable to stay on the field any longer, Mitre returned with some of his troops to restore order at home. His notion of building a nation through a crucible of fire was going up in smoke, and the newly spun fabric of the Argentine state was raveling.

Mitre finally returned to the battlefront in August 1867, but his time in the field was short-lived. A rift with the Brazilian military commander, the Duke of Caixas, forced him to return once more to Buenos Aires. He was also facing the end of his presidential term, and he could no longer stay in command. Tired of Mitre's military tactics, the Brazilian commander decided to bypass the major Paraguayan fortifications and lay direct siege on the capital city of Asuncion in order to end the conflict. The plan worked well, and the city fell on January 1, 1869. The allies sacked the capital, raping and pillaging along the way. Orders were given to kill all men and boys above the age of twelve. Solano Lopez escaped into the hinterland, but he was hunted down in the dense forests of the Chaco and killed at Cerro Cora in March of 1870.[27]

The war devastated Paraguay. The country lost much of its territory, more than half of its population, and all of its industry. Paraguay would never emerge from the ashes of the War of the Triple Alliance; instead, it became one of the poorest and most backward states of the continent. However, the conflict helped Argentina find a common purpose. Although some Argentines were strongly opposed to the campaign, it gave the fledgling nation an important victory and a sense

27 William Jeffrey, *Mitre and Argentina* (New York: Library Publisher, 1952), 220.

of self-esteem.[28] The fact that Urquiza did not use the war as a pretext to commence a new rebellion against Buenos Aires—perhaps because he was too busy pursuing his own commercial interests—marked an important milestone. Given the great deal of resentment against Brazil by the population of Entre Rios and Corrientes, he could have easily started a new campaign against Buenos Aires. Yet, Urquiza remained loyal, raising troops and making a tidy little profit along the way.[29] The War of the Triple Alliance set the stage for Argentina's next president, Domingo Faustino Sarmiento—a leader whose ideas would loom large in the nation's imagination.

Sarmiento was a close friend and ally of Mitre. Indeed, Mitre chose him as his successor when Vice President Marcos Paz died suddenly. Sarmiento was born in the northern province of San Juan to a modest family. The errant youth was insolent, but he was also brilliant and autodidactic. His hot temper and piquant pen soon forced him into exile in Chile where he met Mitre. The two young men became fast friends and worked as journalists. Like his predecessor, Sarmiento was strongly opposed to the tyranny of Rosas. He constantly wrote editorial attacks against the barbaric policies of the Argentine dictator. Soon he became a liability for the Chilean government, and they decided to send him abroad to Europe and the United States to study foreign educational systems. The Chilean government was afraid that his constant tirades against Rosas would eventually produce a reprisal from the Argentine government. Yet, as Urquiza was preparing his

---

28 José Campobassi, *Sarmiento y Mitre: Hombres de Mayo y Caseros* (Buenos Aires: Editorial Losada, 1952), 13.

29 Uruquiza's cooperation in the War of the Triple Alliance fueled hatred from the Federalists and sealed his assassination.

final campaign against Rosas, the indefatigable Sarmiento crossed the Andes to participate in the final attack. He was immediately commissioned to chronicle the operation and participated in the pivotal Battle of Caseros—thus reveling in Rosas's inglorious defeat. Like Mitre, his hatred was against the dictator and not against the Unitarian cause. After the dust settled, Sarmiento switched sides and joined forces with Buenos Aires.

Sarmiento did not rise to national prominence for his actions or policies, but for his ideals. The gist of his argument was in his masterpiece, *Facundo: Civilization and Barbarism.*[30] The book focused on the life of Facundo Quiroga, a bloody caudillo who terrorized the provinces during the first two decades after independence. Sarmiento argued that the inherent barbarism of his countrymen was due to the rugged nature of the Latin American countryside. In other words, the harsh elements that Argentine leaders such as Quiroga and Rosas had to endure forced them to adopt autocratic means. However, Argentina needed to move into a new phase of development that allowed it to bring civilization through education, immigration, and technology. The modernization of the Argentine state became the central theme of Sarmiento's administration. He felt that the taming of the gaucho was achieved only by the civilizing leadership of a great metropolis. In the case of Argentina, the only cosmopolitan area that could play such an important role was Buenos Aires.

Sarmiento's main political objective was to continue with the process of national consolidation by preserving the integrity of the state. Unlike many other countries that sought to

---

30 Domingo Faustino Sarmiento, *Civilization and Barbarism,* trans. Kathleen Ross (Berkeley: University of California Press, 2003).

preserve the constitutional rights of individuals, the early Argentine leaders were more focused on protecting the institutional equilibrium that was hammered out in the battles of Cepeda, Caseros, and Pavon. As an overarching theme, the rights of individuals would not appear on the national agenda until the twenty-first century. Hence, Sarmiento was not shy about using authoritarian means to get his policies across.[31] He ruthlessly put down armed uprisings, particularly by brigands and gauchos. His second objective was the modernization of the state. To do so, Sarmiento tapped the vast experiences he had accumulated in his travels abroad. He established the first academy of science and invited foreign academics and scholars to staff the national institute. He launched the first national census and expanded the telegraph and railroad networks. Sarmiento also modernized the country's basic education system. He commissioned more than eight hundred schools, including high schools and colleges for each of the provinces. The vestiges of Sarmiento's work are reflected in the country's literacy rate of 97 percent, which remains the highest in Latin America. He also encouraged European immigration in order to improve the country's educational traditions and social values.[32] Of course, not all Argentines were so dismissive of the gauchos. As Sarmiento was finishing his term in office, José Hernandez was putting the finishing touches on *Martin Fierro*, a paean to the rugged men of the pampas. Argentina would always have a dichotomy between its love of civilization and its penchant

---

31 Susana Villavicencio, *Sarmiento y La Nacion Civica* (Buenos Aires: Universidad de Buenos Aires, 2008), 27.

32 Mauricio Lebedinsky, *Sarmiento, Más alla de la Educacion* (Buenos Aires: Capital Intelectual, 2009), 106-109.

for barbarism. It would revel in its European roots while having a reckless disregard for the established rules of business, international law, and human rights.

With a sense of national identity rising out of Mitre's war against Paraguay and Sarmiento's crusade against barbarism, Julio Argentino Roca's conquest of the desert culminated the consolidation of the Argentine nation. In contrast to Mitre and Sarmiento, who were formed during the revolution, Roca was born in 1843—in the midst of the civil war. Like his predecessors, he did not grow up in the great metropolis. Roca was from Tucuman, in the northern reaches of the country. Like Mitre and Sarmiento, Roca took up arms against Buenos Aires, but later switched sides to join the Unitarian cause.

Roca's rise to national prominence occurred during the so-called Campaign of the Desert, when his troops conquered a large swath of the country's southern territories. As the nineteenth century wore on, it became clear that the future of Argentina lay to the south. The Northern provinces did not have the climatic or soil conditions needed to participate in the growing agricultural boom that was transforming the pampas.[33] New shipping technologies were reducing freight times and allowing the shipment of grains and chilled beef. Quantum leaps in textile technologies also fed the ferocious demand for wool. As a result, the rich landowners of Buenos Aires were hungry for more pastures and farmland to expand their agrarian operations. They hired bands of gauchos to drive the indigenous population away, but the encroachment of Indian lands triggered a backlash. Raiding

33 Roberto Cortes Conde, *The First Stages of Modernization in Spanish America* (New York: Harper & Row, 1974), 117.

parties attacked settlements. They ransacked *estancias* and made off with women and children. As a result, the government increased its forces on the frontier.

President Nicolas Avellaneda ordered the construction of new fortifications and barriers to keep the indigenous population at bay. Nevertheless, the frontier towns remained under attack. The government's initial idea was to move the Indian population farther south, but they resisted. The southern latitudes of Argentina are cold, arid, and inhospitable. Faced with greater resistance, Buenos Aires decided to intensify the campaign. In 1877, President Avellaneda appointed Julio Argentino Roca to lead a new military expedition. Roca was already an established figure on the national stage. He distinguished himself during the War of the Triple Alliance, and soon employed many of the same ruthless techniques in the Campaign of the Desert.

Like the grasslands of the North American Great Plains, the pampas were considered virtual deserts. However, they were still able to support the nomadic hunting tribes that wandered aimlessly across the empty expanse. Without any towns or citadels to attack, Roca decided that the only way to defeat the indigenous population was to sweep them up in a coordinated campaign. Starting from the large cities of Mendoza, Cordoba, and Santa Fe, Roca's cavalry stretched into a long line and annihilated everything in its path. More than two thousand Indians were killed and fourteen thousand captured. The culmination of the military campaign allowed the triumphant Roca to return to Buenos Aires and launch his successful bid for the presidency. Although his actions would be criminal in the modern age, Roca was hailed as a national hero—allowing the country to expand its frontier and emerge as one of the most promising states of the twentieth century.

This, indeed, was an age of conquest, when the new territories of the United States, Russia, Australia, and Canada annexed their hinterland, displaying complete disregard for existing societies. The Tournament of Shadows, for example, was a contest between Russia and Great Britain for the control of Central Asia, which allowed the former to expand its empire to the Pacific by practically enslaving scores of civilizations. Many of the richest families in Russia made their fortunes from mining and farming concessions that were bequeathed by the Czar in Siberia and the Far East. Canada also undertook military campaigns to subjugate the indigenous population of Saskatchewan and Alberta. The drive for land was driven by the need for more commodities. Technological advances in transportation, communications, and manufacturing brought the global economy together, transforming Europe's Industrial Revolution into a global phenomenon.

All across the world, there was a mad dash for commodities. Explorers probed deep into the Australian outback in search of precious metals. Commercial adventurers pushed into the Amazon to tap its enormous bounty of mineral deposits and agricultural diversity. The rubber boom at the end of the nineteenth century transformed the map of South America, leading to border skirmishes between Brazil, Peru, Colombia, and Bolivia. Africa was ripped apart by the race for natural resources. The European powers carved up the continent without any regard for the existing demographic dispersion, in the process dooming the continent to two centuries of civil war and abject poverty. Therefore, Roca's military campaign was no different from the events that were reshaping the globe. There was a burning desire for natural resources that ignored all other considerations.

Roca's military campaign marked a turning point for the Argentine economy. The disastrous War of the Triple Alliance exhausted the country's resources and left the government deep in debt. However, Roca's efforts boosted the country's economic outlook by annexing thousands of square kilometers of new farmland that would soon be placed into production. Unfortunately, it also sowed the seeds for future political problems.

In order to finance the campaign, the government sold large parcels of land to investors, merchants, and landowners. The land was offered at deep discounts. As a result, these individuals dramatically expanded their wealth and power, thus allowing them to tighten their control over the political apparatus. Unlike the conquest of the Great Plains of North America, whereby the land was subdivided into small lots for poor farmers and immigrants, the annexation of the southern pampas led to an unprecedented transfer of wealth. It created a landed aristocracy that would dominate the national agenda for the next century.

In sum, Mitre's war against Paraguay unified the nation under a single banner. Sarmiento's struggle against barbarism established the country's tradition of academic excellence. Meanwhile, Roca's drive against the Indians expanded the nation's frontiers. The ploughs and railroads that trailed in the soldiers' wake would mark the start of a period of great prosperity. As was the case with the formation of the early colonies and the struggle for independence, geography played a critical role in creating the nation's identity.

The Red Tide

The consolidation of the Argentine nation coincided with a large inflow of foreign resources. Generous concessions were given to railway developers to penetrate deep into the pampas. At first, the government gave developers half a league (or one and a half miles) on either side of the tracks in lieu of subsidies, as well as a rate of return of at least 7 percent.[34] At the same time, Argentina was enjoying an unprecedented period of immigration, as millions fled persecution and wars in Southern and Eastern Europe. Government agents were sent abroad with the promise of land, temporary lodging, and boundless opportunities.[35] Arrivals exploded fortyfold between 1860 and 1880.[36] The immigrants who went to

34 Collin Lewis, *British Railways in Argentina 1857-1914* (London: University of London, 1983), p.32 .

35 Roberto Cortes Conde, *The First Stages of Modernization of Spanish America* (New York: Harper & Row, 1974), 128.

36 Roberto Cortes Condes, *The First Stages of Modernization in Spanish America* (New York: Harper & Row, 1974), 129.

Argentina were part of the same wave that went to the shores of the United States and Australia. Brazil, Chile, Peru, and Venezuela witnessed an influx of people who brought skills, capital, and cultural diversity. Yet, they also brought new political ideas about the organization of society, particularly the ideologies of communism, socialism, and anarchism that had sprouted throughout Europe and morphed into a virtual red tide as the Argentine economy grew.

The advent of the industrial revolution heralded the start of a new era of economic organization, as technology augmented human labor to boost output. However, the new processes required a great deal of capital in order to purchase machinery, build factories, and hire workers. Gone were the cottage industries of tradesmen who assembled the basic goods needed for everyday life. However, the new industries were more sensitive to the random factors that affected business conditions, such as weather, diseases, and wars. These elements coalesced into the business cycle, which dictated operating revenues and costs. With a need to maintain a positive return on capital, business leaders were forced to trim outlays during the downward phase of the cycle. Labor was one of the inputs that were easy to adjust. The relative balance of power in favor of the capitalist versus individual employees made it simple to adjust wages during periods of declining output. Workers soon realized that the only way they could counter such inequitable conditions was by banding together into organized groups. The skewed distribution of wealth produced by capitalism forced some theorists to look for alternative forms of economic organization.

As workers were seeking to improve their ability to negotiate by banding together collectively, Western civilization was facing an existential crisis. The advances in science allowed society to take greater control over its environment and destiny. As a result, the importance of religion diminished. In addition to providing spiritual guidance, religion was used to explain the mysteries of nature. People prayed for rain, prosperity, and health in the hope that divine intervention would change the course of events. However, the acceleration of the sciences allowed society to control the environment through modern farming techniques, business practices, and medicine. In other words, technology slowly began replacing God and religion. Friedrich Nietzsche's concept of superman was not the portrayal of an individual with remarkable powers, but the ability of man to dominate the course of nature.

Scientists and scholars looked for other ways to harness the meandering of nature, including economics. No longer content with allowing the business cycle to run through its violent spasms of expansion and contraction, which always led to social unrest, they looked for ways to smooth the oscillations in the same way that engineers were able to counteract the damages produced by changes in weather patterns by controlling rivers through dams and irrigation systems. They rejected the basic tenet of classical economics, which is to examine the mechanics of the business cycle without managing it. Instead, they looked for ways to harness and control it. Known as neoclassical economists, these theorists were divided into several branches. Two of the first critics of the classical model were Karl Marx and Friedrich Engel.

Marx and Engel argued that the fundamental problem with the free market was that the factors of production were owned by individuals who would always enjoy a dispropor-tionate power over workers. Therefore, the way to smooth out the business cycle was to pass the ownership of industry to the state, which would in turn be controlled by the workers. Under communism, capital would be jointly owned and con-trolled, thus allowing everyone to equally absorb the impact of the variations in the business cycle and avert large adjust-ments in employment and wages. Likewise, society would enjoy all of the economic benefits produced by capital.

A less severe form of communism was socialism. It did not advocate the entire transfer of industry and capital to the state. Instead, it recommended a mixed arrangement, whereby the government played an important role in creating a more level playing field between capitalists and labor. This could be done through the control of strategic industries, particularly in sectors that could monopolize the competi-tion and generate disproportionate returns—such as utilities. The government could play an important role in managing labor relations and making sure that negotiations were fair and equitable. It could also tax the capitalist class to provide workers with greater benefits during periods of economic downturns.

As these theories were discussed during the first half of the nineteenth century, it became clear that the capitalist class would not cooperate. Any transformation would require violence and social unrest, which led to the rise of a third group known as the anarchists. They argued that the only way to achieve social change was through armed conflict. There were several variations of anarchism. Some advocated the complete destruction of modern society to wipe the slate clean and start all over again. Others wanted to use violence in order to compel society to adopt a more equitable form of economic organization, such as communism or social-ism. Anarchists resorted to armed uprisings, bombings, and assassinations. Obviously, they were considered danger-ous subversives and were quickly incarcerated or deported. Many of these ideologists found themselves forced onto ves-sels destined for the United States and Argentina, where they put many of their ideas into practice.

The massive inflow of immigrants and ideas coincided with a burst of industrialization in Argentina. Further advances in shipping technology introduced steam-powered vessels, which allowed faster transportation of climate-controlled per-ishable goods. Moreover, freight lines were able to boost their profitability by taking immigrants on one leg of the journey and carrying cargo on the return. The arrival of transoceanic telegraph lines allowed Argentina to improve its connection with the rest of the world, thus facilitating the integration of business operations. At the same time, the proliferation of railroad lines deep into the pampas permitted farmers in the hinterland to bring more products to market. Between 1880 and 1890, the operational mileage of Argentine rail-roads expanded fourfold to 5,069 miles.[37] All of these new operations required additional labor to work the farms, run the railroads, and manage the slaughterhouses. Therefore, in the 1880s, Argentina witnessed a period of high economic growth marked by ample credit and strong capital inflows.

Of the three main factors of production, land, labor, and capital, Argentina was well endowed with the first. The scar-city of labor and capital had not been a problem during its

---

37 Collin Lewis, *British Railways in Argentina 1857-1914* (London: University of London, 1983), 68.

initial development. There was sufficient labor and capital for the dominant economic activities of the time. Moreover, land had always been abundant in Argentina. The bounty of territory was what allowed the first Argentine industries to develop, by acting as suppliers to the miners of Potosi. However, the modernization of the agrarian industry required skilled labor and a great deal of capital. Fortunately, many of the newly arrived immigrants were well educated and had industrial experience. Likewise, the government's policies of promoting investment boosted foreign capital inflows. Between 1880 and 1890, for example, British investment jumped sevenfold.[38] Much of it went into railroads, which doubled the length of track to 10,292 miles, at a total investment of £105 million.[39] In addition to railroads, capital poured into new gas, water, and electricity projects, as well as the construction of deepwater ports, such as Puerto Madero in Buenos Aires. Consequently, the country was able to modernize.

President Roca's economic policies were very successful, and they were continued by his successor, Miguel Angel Juarez Celman, who was elected in 1886. He hailed from Cordoba and was Roca's brother-in-law. Juarez Celman was an integral member of the political machine that emerged during the war. Known as the National Autonomous Party (PAN), it was akin to many of the other political machines that were appearing across the planet, such as Tammany Hall. The PAN took advantage of the growing nexus between industry and politics by engendering favorable legislation while exacting

---

38 Roberto Cortes Conde, *The First Stages of Modernization in Spanish America* (New York: Harper & Row, 1974), 134.

39 Collin Lewis, *British Railways in Argentina 1857-1914* (London: University of London, 1983), 68.

economic patronage. State assets, for example, were sold to close friends and associates, allowing new fortunes to be amassed.

Although the Argentine economy was doing well under Juarez Celman, the government was afraid that it would not have sufficient gold reserves to service its foreign obligations. Therefore, the government introduced a new monetary system in 1887. The program allowed local banks to issue paper currency if they deposited part of the funds, in the form of gold or a convertible foreign currency, at the central bank. At the same time, the government introduced capital controls to limit the convertibility of the currency in order to husband its reserves. As a result, the value of the Argentine currency began to appreciate. Private and provincial banks eventually realized that they could take out foreign loans and deposit the proceeds at the central bank, and in doing so, they could issue a greater number of notes. The result was the overheating of the Argentine economy, the sharp deterioration of the country's balance of payments, and an explosive growth in foreign obligations.

In 1890, the situation came to a head. Despite the horrible experience that Baring Brothers suffered during its first loan to Argentina and the troubled loans that were issued during the Paraguay War and the Campaign of the Desert, that London financial institution was once more the country's main banker. It underwrote countless loans and bonds for Argentine entities. However, by 1889, the appetite for Argentina was waning, and a bond issue for a new waterworks project failed. At the start of 1890, investment into Argentina evaporated. Faced with the servicing needs of the railroad guarantees, a large trade deficit, and a tremendous amount of private and provincial bank loans, the government no longer had the resources to pay its foreign debt.[40] The default pushed the country into a deep economic crisis as banks failed, savings were wiped out, and businesses lost all access to credit. The government was forced to slash spending, and businesses were obliged to fire workers and reduce wages. It was out of the embers of the financial crisis of 1890 that the radical labor ideas that were festering below the surface finally found the light of day.

As the economic crisis deepened, a new political youth movement gained prominence. Known as the Civic Union, the members railed against the corrupt interconnection between business and politics. Mitre acted as a leader of the movement, but his participation was duplicitous, since his sole interest was to return to power. He was happy to stay in the background where he could play a powerful yet shadowy role. Therefore, the leadership of the movement was passed to an aspiring lawyer named Leandro N. Alem. Calling for an end to the administration of Juarez Celman, Alem organized an armed uprising in July 1890, known as the Revolution of the Park. Mitre contributed by convincing several military groups to mutiny in order to help the rebels, including a squadron of naval warships that opened fire on Buenos Aires.

Alem was a native of Buenos Aires and was a distinguished military veteran who had participated in the Battles of Cepeda and Pavon. He later studied law and entered politics. Alem was a passionate ideologue along the traditions of Belgrano, Moreno, and Castelli. He believed that Argentina needed political reforms to combat the interests that control-

---

40 David Rock, *Argentina 1516-1987* (Los Angeles: University of California Press, 1987), 157-159.

led the economy and prevented the general population from enjoying the fruits of its growing prosperity.

Alem was betrayed by Mitre, who cut a secret deal with Roca to force Juarez Celman to step down and pass the presidential baton to Vice President Carlos Pellegrini. Once his term was finished, Roca would endorse Mitre for a return to office. However, nothing was done to address the economic inequities. Indeed, Mitre and Roca vowed to contain Alem and his radical movement. Less than a month after the uprising, Juarez Celman resigned and Pellegrini was sworn in. Alem quickly realized what had happened and split away, forming the radical faction of the Civic Union. The party became known as the UCR or Radicals, and it was the first ideologically based political party in Argentina. Unlike the previous political parties, which represented the interests of Buenos Aires and the provinces, the UCR was much more of a reformist platform that promoted universal suffrage and the elimination of corruption.

At the same time, social unrest was on the rise. Millions of immigrants were collecting in the neighborhoods of Buenos Aires, Rosario, and Cordoba. The economic crisis forced businesses and farms to fire workers, and there were scarce opportunities for the new arrivals. Moreover, the concentration of wealth within the hands of the landed aristocracy prevented the dispersion of resources. Most of the new arrivals had nowhere to go other than the teeming ghettos. Melancholy set in among the working people, who felt marooned in a godforsaken land that sat on the opposite side of the globe from the lands they called home. The sadness was manifested in the music, melodies, and dance movements that became known as tangos. This style of music was born in the brothels and canteens of the working class and incorporated instruments and rhythms from Southern and Eastern Europe that expressed the musicians' longing for a better life.

However, not everyone was suffering to the same extent. The crisis of 1890 passed quickly for the landed aristocracy, allowing the Gilded Age to arrive in its full glory. Immense wealth was showered upon the land barons, industrialists, and politicians, permitting them to build Belle Epoque palaces along the grand avenues of Recoleta. Similar structures were sprouting from the ground in New York, Chicago, Santiago, Shanghai, and Saint Petersburg. The wealthy enjoyed access to the latest technology and pleasures, including private train cars and luxurious steam ships. As the wage gap between the classes soared, workers banded together to protest the miserable factory and living conditions. Argentine railroad workers were among the first to form syndicates to represent their interests and negotiate with management. Given the nature of the railway industry, organizers were able to move around and spread ideas, thus boosting their ability to unify.[41] They used pamphlets, newspapers, and rallies to educate workers. In 1887, Argentine railroad engineers established the Fraternity, which initiated its first labor action in 1888. The following year, they went on strike for four months demanding better pay, shorter workweeks, and overtime pay. Other groups, such as stevedores, deckhands, and meat packers, were also starting to unite. The ghettos were becoming incubators for radical ideas. Mainly led by anarchists, the various unions began to cooperate, and in 1901, they amalgamated into the Argentine Workers'

41 Joel Horowitz, *Argentina's Radical Party and Popular Mobilization, 1916-1930* (University Park: Pennsylvania State University Press, 2008), 121.

Federation (FOA), which represented more than fifty unions and ten thousand workers.[42]

The Argentine government quickly responded to the organized labor threat. Realizing that the insubordination was led by newly arrived communists, they passed the Law of Residency. This allowed government agents to deport immigrants deemed subversive back to their countries of origin. The implementation of the law was practically a death sentence to many of the activists because they had escaped persecution in their home countries, and now they were wanted by their governments. FOA retaliated by calling a general strike in 1902, which paralyzed the economy.[43] The government was forced to declare martial law to suppress the labor action, but it was clear that a new political power had been unleashed.

As the new social movements became better organized, the activists became more disruptive, which forced the government to counter with stronger measures. As a result, the two sides became increasingly violent. Activist newspaper offices were sacked, and government officials were assassinated. Against this background, the UCR took advantage of the new social tensions by bending them to its own political ambition.

The Radicals had been cast adrift in 1896 when their founder, Alem, committed suicide. He was deeply troubled by the internal rifts within the movement and the intransigence of the government, and by his own personal financial problems. Upon his death, the reins of the party were picked

---

42 Felix Luna, *Conflictos en la Argentina Prospera* (Buenos Aires: Editorial Planeta, 2000), 53.

43 Joel Horowitz, *Argentina's Radical Party and Popular Mobilization, 1916-1930* (University Park: Pennsylvania State University Press, 2008), 18.

up by his nephew, Hipolito Yrigoyen. Like his uncle, he was highly idealistic, but he was much more pragmatic and ambitious. Yrigoyen was quick to compromise in order to resolve problems, and he had a burning desire for power.

At first, the Radicals had very little to do with the nascent labor movement. Their core constituency was the members of the middle class who were disaffected by the deep corruption of the political system. The great fortunes had produced a rigid stratification of the social structure.[44] In other words, the Radicals were not associated with the workers who were taking to the streets. Nevertheless, as the labor movement gained power, Yrigoyen increased his association with the less extreme labor elements, such as the socialists. The passage of the Saenz-Peña Law in 1912, which provided universal, secret, and mandatory suffrage, expanded the electorate base dramatically. Not everyone was allowed to vote. It enfranchised naturalized males, who completed their compulsory military service. Not only did this leave women out of the equation; it also excluded most immigrants. Nevertheless, it forced the Radicals to widen their appeal to the lower classes. Bolstered by the new law, the Radicals began to win elections, and Yrigoyen was swept into the presidency in 1916, culminating a prolonged struggle for more democracy.

The passage of the Saenz-Peña Law and the election of Yrigoyen marked a new schism in Argentine politics. In addition to the division between the conservative and liberal factions, and the rivalry between Buenos Aires and the provinces, the struggle between the classes would be another important

---

44 David Rock, *Politics in Argentina 1890-1930: The Rise and Fall of Radicalism* (Cambridge: Cambridge University Press, 1975), 49.

dimension of the Argentine political system. Given that most of the urban masses resided in the greater Buenos Aires area, it added more credence to the notion that whoever ruled the port dominated the nation. However, the situation was no longer just an issue of who controlled the customs house; it was the representation of the urban poor. As a result, Argentina's development would take a new direction. It would begin to move toward a form of corporatist populism that would fundamentally transform the structure of the economy.

The Rise of the Corporatist State

The First World War marked the apogee of Argentina's export-oriented model. The country sold grains, meats, and wool to the belligerents, amassing a disproportionate level of international reserves. However, important changes were taking place below the surface. The organization of labor groups into well-disciplined syndicates significantly increased the negotiating capabilities of workers, thus affecting the profitability of business operations. Likewise, the passage of the Saenz-Peña Law led to the election of President Hipolito Yrigoyen, which marked the emergence of a new political leader who would no longer be the mouthpiece of the landed aristocracy. These events unleashed forces that ultimately transformed the Argentine state, but the changes were slow in coming. The Congress, particularly the Senate, was still in the hands of the landed aristocracy, and they controlled most of the country's major institutions, such as the military and the judiciary. In a way, this was a new manifestation of the struggle between Buenos Aires and the provinces, since the provinces held many more senate seats than the capital city. Nevertheless, the transformation enhanced the power of Buenos Aires—but in a new way.

Although the global conflict allowed the Argentine economy to do well, it also highlighted several of its flaws. Principally, it showed the limits of concentrating in a few sectors. Argentina is often criticized for its lack of industrialization, but that is not true. The Argentine economy enjoyed a high degree of industrialization at the end of the nineteenth century. However, it was not focused on the production of manufactured goods. It was dedicated to the processing of food and raw materials, such as beef, mutton, wool, and hides. Nevertheless, the economy was still industrialized. Railroads sped products to market. Mechanized combines worked the land. Large meatpacking facilities prepared carcasses for shipment, and sophisticated ports warehoused goods and loaded cargo ships. The country's logistics, communications, and financing capabilities were among the best in the world. Unfortunately, the lack of manufacturing became evident during the conflict when the belligerents redirected most of their efforts toward the preparation of munitions and equipment. As the war deepened, imported goods became scarce, and economic activity dropped as the country ran out of spare parts and capital goods.

To make matters worse, the unending demand for raw materials by the belligerents not only pushed up food prices, but the scarcity of imported goods sent inflation soaring in Argentina.[45] Unfortunately, the end of the fighting did not improve things. European economies were ruined by the conflict. Germany and Austria were bankrupt, Britain was in shambles, and Russia had collapsed into civil war. The United States, which emerged physically unscathed from the conflict, was a major exporter of the same agricultural products produced by Argentina. In other words, the two countries were competitors. Therefore, the United States refused to open its booming markets to Argentine products. At the same time, US exports of capital goods as well as manufactured goods such as automobiles and appliances were gaining ground within the Argentine domestic market. Faced with declining trade flows and higher inflation, the economy entered into a period of stagflation, which heightened the level of social unrest.

In January 1919, a strike at the Vasena metallurgical factory in Buenos Aires turned violent, and a young officer was slain.[46] The police retaliated the next day by ambushing the strikers and killing four people. As a result, the labor unions called a national strike that brought the country to a halt. Witnessing the chaos in Russia, where a bread riot a year earlier had brought down the czar, the governing class and the economic elites were afraid that they could fall victim to a similar fate. Hence, they made a commitment to take on a much harsher stance against labor uprisings. Clandestine paramilitary squads known as the Asociación Nacional del Trabajo (the National Association for Work) began attacking labor

---

45 Carl Solberg, *Oil and Nationalism in Argentina* (Stanford: Stanford University Press, 1979), 22.

46 David Rock, *Politics in Argentina: 1890-1930. The Rise and Fall of the Radicalism* (Cambridge: Cambridge University Press, 1975), 162.

leaders, newspaper reporters, and activists. The bloody confrontation became known as la Semana Tragica (the Tragic Week). What was interesting was that the incident took place during Yrigoyen's government. Soon, a labor uprising in the Province of Santa Cruz would turn into one of the bloodiest massacres in Argentine history.

Although the landed aristocracy made off with the spoils from the Campaign of the Desert, the territory south of the Rio Negro was still up for grabs. The land north of the river was arable, and it was converted into pastures for cattle ranching and grain fields. The land farther south was barren, and it was left to the survivors of the campaign. The region was known as Patagonia. It was virtually a no-man's-land, with scarce natural resources. Interestingly, the name Patagonia was christened by Ferdinand Magellan as he threaded his way around the southern tip of South America en route to the Pacific. The Indians he encountered had very large feet, and he called the territory "the land of big feet"—Patagonia. Several centuries later, ranchers learned that the hardscrabble land was suitable for sheep farming. With cheap land at its disposal, a handful of immigrant families, among them a Russian-German Jewish family called the Brauns, purchased large tracts to raise sheep and produce wool.[47] Within a generation, the Brauns became one of the wealthiest families in the world. They controlled much of the globe's wool production, and the demand for wool grew sharply during the First World War. It was needed to produce the garments to clothe the soldiers who were fighting in the frigid battlefronts of Northern Europe. The demand for wool was so high that it became known as White Gold. Yet, after the war, prices

---

47 Bayer, Osvaldo. *Patagonia Rebelde.* México, (D.F.: Editorial Nueva Imagen, 1980), 13.

plunged as demand collapsed. As a result, the factories and farms in Patagonia were forced to cut back on labor costs. Workers rose in protest, took over farms, and held hostages. Buenos Aires quickly dispatched the 10th Cavalry Regiment, led by Colonel Hector Benigno Varela, to put down the rebellion. Upon his arrival, Colonel Varela demanded the unconditional surrender of the subversives. The strikers debated the situation and decided to break into two factions, with one of them surrendering and the other escaping across the Andes into Chile. Upon turning themselves in, the strikers were gunned down. The group of prisoners consisted of fifteen hundred workers. Prior to being executed, they were disposed of their personal belongings and forced to dig their own graves. After his return to Buenos Aires, instead of being persecuted for his crimes, Colonel Varela was praised and decorated for his actions. This incident marked the last chapter of the first Yrigoyen administration and put the Radicals at loggerheads with the labor unions. It also marked the start of a sad tradition in Argentine history: that of using the military to resolve incidents of civil unrest, which set the precedent for the military to assume a direct role in political matters thereafter.[48]

In the past, the military rarely participated in domestic political disputes. Some military units played an active role in the Revolution of the Park. However, those were mutinous elements. They were never directed by the high command. Argentine militias were involved in various civilian engagements, but the military leadership had set itself apart from the political process ever since San Martin's refusal to abandon

---

48 David Rock, *Argentina 1516-1987* (Los Angeles: University of California Press, 1987), 202-203.

his campaign against Spain to defend the Unitarians against the Federalists. Ironically, Argentina's first democratically elected president opened the door to active participation by the military. Unfortunately, Yrigoyen's decision would have dark consequences for the next sixty years.

Despite establishing such an ominous precedent at the end of his term, President Yrigoyen also founded an important institution that would have a lasting legacy on the country's economic development. In 1922, he signed a decree creating the national oil company, Yacimientos Petrolíferos Fiscales (YPF). The state-owned oil company was born out of the difficulties of the First World War. In addition to the lack of imported manufactured goods and capital equipment, Argentina suffered severe shortages of oil and coal. The Allied countries, which included several of the largest energy exporters in the world, halted embarkations during the conflict. The United States, for example, restricted the export of oil drilling equipment, and Great Britain placed a total embargo on coal exports. This severely undermined the Argentine economy, forcing the government to look for alternative sources of domestic energy. Fortunately, oil was discovered in Argentina on the eve of the conflict. In 1907, Standard Oil of New Jersey struck oil in Commodoro Rivadavia. Unfortunately, the announcement was not welcomed. There was a general sense of resentment against the United States because of its inequitable trade policies. Argentina wanted to rely less on foreign-owned energy companies, particularly North American ones. This proved to be a powerful incentive to create its own domestic variant. Fortunately, YPF started on the right foot. Several significant fields were soon found in the provinces of Salta, Neuquén, and Mendoza. Government support for YPF would continue under President Yrigoyen's successor, Marcelo T. Alvear—another member of the Radical Party. Argentine hydrocarbon output rose steadily during the middle part of the 1920s, and the company registered a quantum leap at the end of the decade.

One of the reasons for YPF's strong performance was its initial leadership. The company's first director-general was Enrique Mosconi, a military aviator with extensive experience in engineering and construction. He sought to create a vertically integrated operation that ranged from exploration and production to refinement and distribution. He was quick to realize that the real value of the oil industry was not in the extraction process but in refining and distribution. To that end, he built Argentina's first refinery in the town of La Plata in 1925, and he established a national network of gasoline distributors. By 1928, YPF had a chain of 912 gasoline stations throughout the country.

Mosconi pursued a program that was national in scope, bringing resources and people to far-flung reaches of the country. In the process, he built new towns for the workers, complete with homes, schools, and medical facilities. He paved roads to bring in supplies and take out oil. Cooperatives were established to provide families with food and goods. YPF began to play an important role in the country's development. It was evident that the use of a state-owned enterprise (SOE) such as YPF could play an important economic part in modernizing the country while creating high-paying jobs.

The issue of YPF took center stage in 1928, as former President Yrigoyen prepared for a second term. He campaigned on a platform of nationalizing the entire oil sector and putting it under the control of YPF. In addition to bringing the industry into the hands of a state-owned company, it also reignited the old conflict between the provinces and Buenos Aires. Oil concessions were initially granted by each of the provinces, not the federal government. Yrigoyen wanted to win a majority in the senate and wrest control of the oil concessions away from the provinces, thus putting the resources firmly in the hands of the federal government. Although Yrigoyen won the presidency, he failed to gain control of the senate. As a result, the law was never changed, and the control of the concessions remained as they were. Once again, the power of Buenos Aires could not stand up to a united provincial front.

Unfortunately, Yrigoyen's second term in office was far from pleasant. A year after he was elected, the New York Stock Exchange crashed heralding the start of the Great Depression. The prices of commodities plunged as factories slashed output and governments resorted to protectionist measures. The Argentine economy was declining from its position of strength in the prewar period. Between 1890 and the start of the First World War, the Argentine economy enjoyed a simultaneous expansion of all three factors of production: an increase in land under cultivation, a boom in foreign investment, and a massive influx of immigrants. Things would improve after the war, but not to the same extent. As the global economy moved into the Roaring Twenties, Argentina's level of economic activity rose and the demand for commodities increased, but the country did not expand the amount of land under cultivation. There was almost no new foreign investment into sectors such as railroads, and the wave of immigration ebbed. The economic policies of

President Alvear were also not as laissez-faire as they were during the Gilded Age of the prewar years. The creation of YPF was clearly a menace to powerful oil interests such as Standard Oil and Shell, both of which trimmed some of their investment projects in Argentina. The same happened to other sectors as workers organized and were able to exact higher wage concessions. Therefore, the Argentine economy was relatively weak as the world slipped into the Great Depression.

Argentina's political situation was also fragile. The landed aristocracy bristled at President Yrigoyen's economic policies. Foreign companies lobbied for political change. Having been praised for the role they played in the subjugation of the labor uprisings in Patagonia, the military leadership felt that they could play a more direct role in stabilizing the country's political situation. Therefore, two army generals, José Felix Uriburu and Agustin P. Justo, plotted a coup. Uriburu was a staunch nationalist with a fascist bent. He admired Mussolini's corporatist approach because it supported a close association between business, labor, and government.[49] Meanwhile, General Justo supported a more democratic approach to government. In September of 1930, he marched onto the presidential residence (Casa Rosada) with a detachment of cadets, and the government quickly fell. President Yrigoyen was eighty years old, infirm, and politically isolated. The Great Depression, resentment by labor unions, and the growing clout of the foreign lobbies hastened his demise. The fact that his administration was thrown over by a group of cadets underscored the fragility of his hold on power.

---

49 Joel Horowitz, *Argentine Unions, the State & the Rise of Peronism* (Berkeley: University of California Press, 1990), 12.

Unfortunately, the coup of 1930 marked the start of a long string of similar events.

The next fifteen years brought an era commonly known as the neoconservative period, whereby the landed aristocracy used the military to reassert political control. Under General Uriburu, communists were jailed, executed, or deported. It was a difficult time for the Argentine economy. The global depression was deeper and longer than anyone imagined. Competitive devaluations and high trade barriers restricted exports. At the same time, the low level of global demand depressed commodity prices, making it difficult for Argentine exporters to revive the bonanza of the prewar years. Fortunately, General Uriburu's dictatorship was short lived. Poor health, a weak economy, and disenchantment with the government's repressive policies forced the government to call elections in 1931. Using fraud and a broad alliance of various political factions, the presidential mantle was passed to General Agustin P. Justo, Uriburu's accomplice in the coup d'état. Initially, Justo was relatively moderate in his approach, and the unions were given some reprieve. However, the nation's focus suddenly shifted north as two neighbors came to blows.

The Chaco Boreal is a barren region that sits at the foothills of the Andes. It is a 245,000-square-kilometer triangle. Two of the sides are prescribed by the Paraguay and Pilcomayo Rivers. Asuncion, the capital of Paraguay, is at the apex, and the base of the triangle is formed by the Parapetí River along the foothills of the Andes. Bereft of water, it is a veritable no-man's-land. Although the region was disputed by Bolivia and Paraguay, Bolivia had a stronger legal claim to it since the territory was once a part of the Audencia of

Charcas in the Viceroyalty of Peru.[50] However, Paraguay had a stronger presence in the Chaco Boreal. Tribes of nomadic Guarani Indians inhabited the region, as well as colonies of Mennonites who had obtained their legal charters from the Paraguayan government. Both Bolivia and Paraguay maintained armed garrisons within the Chaco. The Bolivians had a stronger military presence in the upper third while the Paraguayans had a stronger presence in the lower third, and the middle third was relatively neutral. In reality, there was a general sense of status quo. Unfortunately, the situation changed in 1926 when Standard struck oil in Sanandita, at the foothills of the Andes. The next year, it made a similar find in Camiri, a little farther south. Given the size of the wells, Standard explored nearby regions and made new discoveries in Salta. All eyes immediately shifted to the Chaco, as everyone believed that it would be the next major oil field. On the other side of the border, Royal Dutch Shell was making inroads to the Latin American market. It obtained exploration and drilling rights from the Paraguayan government to develop fields in the Chaco. However, it needed to be sure that its rights would be protected. Therefore, the company pressed the Paraguayan military to gain better control of the region by expelling the Bolivian garrisons.

Bolivia was the bigger country. Its military was better equipped and armed. It was also under pressure from Standard Oil to secure the control of the Chaco. Last of all, it had its own geopolitical interests to gain access to the Paraguay River so that it could ship its products to the Atlantic. In 1883, Bolivia lost its access to the outside world during the War of the Pacific, and it was now landlocked. At the same

50 David Zook, *The Conduct of the Chaco War* (New Haven: Bookman Associates, 1960), 34.

time, Paraguay was a smaller country with fewer men under arms, but it had better leaders. It also had a huge logistical advantage. Asuncion was only three hundred kilometers from the front, and it was able to use the Paraguay River as a virtual highway to mobilize its men and munitions. La Paz was almost two thousand kilometers from the front, with no easy forms of communication and transportation. Finally, the indigenous Bolivian soldiers were used to the cold climate of the altiplano and were unprepared for the heat and diseases of the desert. Meanwhile, the Paraguayan troops were well acclimated to the challenges produced by the tropics.

In an effort to diffuse the crisis, the League of Nations placed an arms embargo on the belligerents. However, the Argentine government managed to ensure that a steady stream of war supplies was delivered to the Paraguayans.[51] British influence was strong in Argentina, and London was able to make sure that its interests were well defended. Argentine landowners also controlled huge tracts of land in the Chaco, much of it used for the growing of yerba mate, an herbal tea that was consumed heavily in Argentina, Paraguay, Uruguay, and Southern Brazil. In the end, the Bolivians were defeated, with a loss of more than sixty thousand men. However, it was a pyrrhic victory for Paraguay. Despite the loss of almost fifty thousand men, Royal Dutch Shell never found oil in the Chaco, and it walked away empty-handed.

The War of the Chaco showed the level of desperation that was driving policies in Bolivia and Paraguay. Argentina, unfortunately, was no different. The landed aristocracy was struggling against adverse global economic conditions, and they were desperate to sell their goods. Great Britain, their

---

51 William Garner, *The Chaco Dispute* (Washington, D.C.: Public Affairs Press, 1966), 85.

traditional market for beef exports, was struggling. Its public debt was 140 percent of GDP, and it was no longer on the gold standard. The British government tried to stabilize the economy by raising the primary surplus to 7 percent of GDP and tightening monetary policy. This put the country on a deflationary trajectory that deepened the recession. Therefore, British consumers had little capacity to purchase Argentine goods. In 1933, the Argentine government tried to counter the problem by entering into a bilateral trade treaty known as the Roca-Runciman Pact. Under the agreement, Argentina was able to continue exporting beef to Britain as long as 85 percent of the production originated in British and American processing plants. In return, the Argentina government slashed tariffs on British imports, particularly manufactured goods and coal. The pact enhanced the growing trend of interventionist policies that started with the creation of YPF. During the prewar economic boom, the state played a minimal role in trade issues. With the exception of creating incentives and guarantees for the building of the railroads, the Argentine government was happy to allow private capital, particularly foreign investors, to make decisions on trade and the allocation of resources. Yet, the state was now playing a more dominant role.

The character of the Argentine economy was also changing. The shortages and hardships imposed by the First World War allowed Argentine entrepreneurs to focus more on manufacturing. Local companies began making advances in metallurgy, machinery, and munitions. As their economic power grew, the companies banded together into confederations that represented their interests. The most prominent of the industrial groups was the Industrial Argentine Union (UIA).

The UIA was in sharp contrast to the main agricultural lobby, Sociedad Rural, which had been in existence since 1866. Both confederations represented the capitalist class, but the latter espoused an open economic model. Meanwhile, the former wanted a closed arrangement. Interestingly, they also had strong social aspects to their institutions. The Sociedad Rural held an annual fair in July, which dated back to 1886. Presidents and politicians were always present at the fair, and it remains a venue for major political announcements. The UIA had its palatial headquarters in the center of the city, and actively promoted studies on economic policies. The competition between these two groups marked a new schism that would repeatedly send tremors throughout the country.

The 1930s were also labeled the Age of Infamy for the rampant corruption and cronyism that defined that decade. Industrialists and the landed aristocracy rammed through favorable legislative measures. At the same time, the electoral advances that were achieved through the ratification of the Saenz-Peña Law were eroded. Electoral fraud was rampant, which allowed a right-wing oligarchy to control the state. Nevertheless, the essential elements of the corporatist state were falling into place. Industrialists, well-organized labor unions, and the growing willingness of the government to intervene in economic matters were now prominent features of the Argentine political apparatus. All that was missing was a political entrepreneur to bring the strands together and coalesce it into a unified movement. That entrepreneur appeared in 1943 in the form of Colonel Juan Domingo Peron.[52]

---

52 James Brennan and Marcelo Rougier, *The Politics of National Capitalism: Peronism and the Argentine Bourgeoisie, 1946-1976* (University Park: Pennsylvania State University Press,

As Argentina was gearing up once more for presidential elections, a left-wing alliance between the Radicals, socialists, and communists, known as the Democratic Union, was poised to sweep the field. The only way that a leftist victory could be averted was through widespread electoral fraud, which would plunge the country into social unrest. This was when the military decided to take matters into its own hands. There was not so much fear that the left would take control. The military was more concerned that the government would be forced to abandon its neutrality in regards to the Second World War.

Argentina aggressively pursued a policy of neutrality during the First World War, and it was doing the same during the second global conflict. By taking a position of neutrality, it could sell agricultural products at inflated prices to all of the belligerents. Moreover, there was a strong affinity between Argentina and Germany. Many German immigrants had arrived at the turn of the century, and cultural ties were deep.

Last of all, there was a strong sense of resentment against the British and Americans. The antipathy against the British was due to their heavy-handed influence in the Argentine economy, and the dislike of the Americans stemmed from their unilateral trade policies. Therefore, the military hierarchy wanted to ensure that the country would not join the fight against the Nazis.

To that end, a group of colonels formed the Working Group for Unification (GOU), a secret society with the aim of defending the military's principle interests, which included resisting the rise of communism and ensuring the country's

2009), 2.

neutrality.[53] The military had also amassed a great deal of power ever since General Uriburu's coup, and by the 1940s, it played a significant role across several important sectors, such as the running of the merchant marine and munitions factories. This was a new form of corporatism that created an economic nexus between the public and private sectors with the military playing a central role. High-ranking officers also held key policy-making positions. That was how Colonel Peron was appointed to the National Labor and Pensions Department (DNT). In reality, the position was not that important, but Peron's political maneuvering resulted in the office being expanded into the Ministry of Labor. He then used the newly minted ministry to catapult himself into the national limelight. Powerful levers were at his disposal, including direct influence over the budding industrial sector, the ability to impose labor agreements on the unions, and the enormous financial resources that were deposited into union pension plans. Yet, instead of working closely with the established labor unions, Peron redirected his policies to benefit the mass of migrant workers who were drifting into the poor suburbs on the outskirts of Buenos Aires.

The Great Depression and the collapse of agricultural prices forced many tenant farmers in the provinces to abandon their lands and decamp for the capital. This was in addition to the immigrant ghettos of La Boca and San Telmo that teamed with people who had failed to move into the interior. The new arrivals were largely unskilled types that Karl Marx

---

53 Joel Horowitz, *Argentine Unions, the State & the Rise of Peronism* (Berkeley: University of California Press, 1990), 22.

and Frederic Engels referred to as the *lumpenproletariat*.[54] For Marxists, these people were rabble who played no role in the transformation of society. Indeed, they were considered a threat since they could be mobilized and used to support political movements. Marx and Engels believed that this was what Napoleon Bonaparte did when he hijacked a legitimate social revolution by mobilizing the nation's rabble to promote his own personal ambitions. It could be argued that Peron did the same thing. Not only did Peron mobilize these immigrants for political events; they became the backbone of his electoral base. He used the powers at his disposal to give them the right to negotiate collectively, and he gave them paid vacations and pension benefits. As a result, Peron emerged as the leading political figure of the time.

Peron was a clear break from the traditional military leader who represented the interests of the landed aristocracy. Argentina's earliest military leaders, particularly San Martin and Belgrano, were idealists who championed a more equitable society. However, Peron was not interested in social revolution. He clearly did not represent the interests of any of the groups that were struggling for more power, such as the traditional labor unions, the socialists, or the industrialists. In fact, he turned his back on all of these groups. Instead, he used the masses to power his political machine. Colloquially, the masses became known as the "little black heads" or *cabecitas negras*. This was a denigrating reference to the dark hair of the people from the interior, with many of them of mestizo birth, who contrasted with the fair-haired citizens of Buenos Aires. Peron transported thousands of *cabecitas*

---

54 Karl Marx and Frederic Engels, *The Communist Manifesto* (London: William Reeves Bookseller, 1888), 18.

negras into the capital and dumped them into the impromptu slums. He paraded them through affluent neighborhoods prior to his political rallies as a form of intimidation. This electoral mass was the new factor that allowed Buenos Aires to retain its political dominance during a period of economic flux. The army of urban poor became the backbone of the Peronist machine, and whoever controlled them ruled the nation. Therefore, like the caudillos who had conquered Buenos Aires in the past, Peron knew that the only way to gain control of the national apparatus was by taking command of Buenos Aires.

As his public persona grew, Peron's position within the military junta also kept rising. Between 1943 and 1946, a revolving door of military dictators passed through the presidency, and Peron soon became the vice president to General Edelmiro Farrell. At the same time, he continued to serve as Minister of Labor and Secretary of War. Peron's public standing was further boosted by his humanitarian efforts to help the victims of a devastating earthquake in the province of San Juan in January 1944, which had left thousands dead and many more homeless. During one of the star-studded events used to promote fundraising for the victims, he met and fell in love with an aspiring actress named Eva Duarte, who quickly caught the public's attention. Peron was a master of the stage. Using the advances in media, he flaunted his relationship with Evita to raise his profile. By 1946, it was clear that Peron was unstoppable. The traditional power groups of the country, particularly the landed aristocracy, were petrified by his growing popularity, and they pressured the more conservative elements of the military to oust him.[55] That is why in October of 1945, Peron was sacked and exiled. The public's reaction was swift. Tens of thousands took to the streets, and the military suddenly realized that the country was on the brink of civil war. Therefore, they decided to repatriate Peron, whereby he launched his presidential campaign. Fighting for survival, the traditional political factions, primarily the Radicals and landed aristocracy, unified under a single political ticket to oppose him. However, it was to no avail, and the charismatic leader was swept into power.

Peron's election put Argentina at a critical juncture. This is a conceptual framework used by social scientists to examine a significant shift in a country's development path.[56] Although Argentina had developed the core institutional elements of a corporatist state, it was still primarily a free-market agricultural-based economy. The start of the Peron presidency would mark an important change in the country's economic model by focusing much more on manufacturing activities. Yet, it is important to stress that Peron was nothing more than a political entrepreneur who took advantage of the opportunities that were at hand. He did not invent Argentina's corporatist model. This was started by Yrigoyen and Uriburu. He wasn't the founder of Argentina's industrialization efforts or labor unions. Those began at the turn of the century. However, he brought the elements together into a singular political movement. He did it to boost his own personal power,

---

55 Joel Horowitz, *Argentina's Radical Party and Popular Mobilization, 1916-1930* (University Park: Pennsylvania State University Press, 2008), 188.

56 Ruth Berins Collier and David Collier, *Shaping the political arena : critical junctures, the labor movement, and regime dynamics in Latin America* (Princeton: Princeton University Press, 1991), 32.

and then he permanently institutionalized his goals by rewriting the constitution in 1949. [57]

The effect of Peron's measures accelerated the industrialization efforts that were already underway. Argentina's industrial output doubled between 1930 and 1949, and imports dropped by three-fourths, as a percentage of GDP.[58] As his political movement strengthened, it is important to note that his relationship with the traditional labor unions deteriorated. The Railroad Federation (UF), for example, paralyzed the country in 1950 with a national strike, which Peron declared illegal, and then he sent the military to repress it.

The start of the Peron presidency also coincided with major changes in the structure of the global economy. In 1947, India declared independence from Great Britain. In 1949, Mao Tze Tung defeated the last Nationalist redoubt in Shanghai and took control of the Chinese mainland. Both governments placed their countries on similar economic trajectories. Although the Indian and Chinese governments were very different, they decided to pursue policies of isolation in order to purge all foreign elements after a century of colonial rule. Through a policy of import substitution industrialization, India imposed severe tariff restrictions on imported goods, including agricultural products. Likewise, Mao's collectivization policies pushed his country into a deep depression. India and China were the most affluent countries at the start of the nineteenth century, boosting the fortunes of commodity producers such as Argentina. Indeed, the initial fortunes of

---

57 Daniel James, *Resistance and Integration: Peronism and the Argentine Working Class, 1946-1976* (Cambridge: Cambridge University Press, 1988), 17.

58 Daniel James, *Resistance and Integration: Peronism and the Argentine Working Class, 1946-1976* (Cambridge: Cambridge University Press, 1988), 8.

Argentina were established due to the role it played in deep-ening Europe's trade ties with Asia. However, by the end of the twentieth century, these two Asian giants had reduced their per capita income levels to those found in sub-Saharan Africa. All commodity producers were severely affected by the changes. China and India represented a quarter of the world's population, and their simultaneous removal from the global economy marked the start of a prolonged downturn in prices of raw materials. The downturn also affected many developed countries that were large commodity producers, such as the United States, Canada, Australia, and even some of the European states. Therefore, these countries protected themselves by imposing high import tariffs on agricultural products and introducing government subsidies to protect domestic farmers. The result was the collapse in global food prices.

This is when Argentina's fractious relationship with the United States became painfully apparent. The troubled ties with the United States was one of several reasons why Argentina remained neutral during the Second World War and waited until the conflict was over before declaring war on Ger-many in March 1945. This infuriated Washington, especially since Brazil was an active member of the alliance and sent an expeditionary force to fight in Italy. United States Ambassa-dor Spruille Braden was a vocal critic of the Argentine foreign policy, and he often launched verbal attacks against Peron.[59] The United States later retaliated against Argentina's neutral-ity by forbidding European nations to import any Argentine products if those nations were receiving aid from the Marshall

---

59 Robert Wesson, *U.S. Influence in Latin America in the 1980s* (Stanford: Hoover Institute Press, 1982), 40.

Plan.[60] Buenos Aires slowly found itself with the wrong comparative advantage and on the wrong side of the new global fence. Furthermore, its deep alliance with Great Britain was coming up shorthanded.

By the end of the war, Britain was facing financial ruin. Beleaguered by huge wartime debts, Parliament passed a nonconvertibility law and froze foreign assets. Argentina had indebted itself since its independence, but by the end of the Second World War, it was a wealthy nation with large sums deposited in British banks. At the same time, Britain held a significant amount of assets in Argentina in the form of railroads, ports, telecommunication companies, and beef processing plants. Therefore, Peron decided to do a debt for equity swap, exchanging the financial assets he had in London and other parts of Europe for physical assets located in Argentina.[61] He nationalized the British railroads, telephone companies, and electricity utilities. Although the nationalization of these companies did not expand the country's level of industrialization, it gave the government a bigger role in key sectors. These SOEs, along with YPF, became the economic foundation of the Peronist system, which allowed the country to become more autarkic and statist in its approach.

Peron's main objective became the management of the new state enterprises. At the same time, Argentina's other traditional economic forces were marginalized by the changes abroad. The UIA never enjoyed a close relationship with Peron. He was more interested in favoring the industries

---

60 James Brennan and Marcelo Rougier, *The Politics of National Capitalism: Peronism and the Argentine Bourgeoisie, 1946-1976* (University Park: Pennsylvania State University Press, 2009), 6.

61 Walter Molano, *The Logic of Privatization* (Westport: Greenwood Press, 1997), 84.

and sectors that he controlled. Hence, the UIA increased its hostility to the regime by becoming an integral part of the opposition movement. Peron often referred to them as the oligarchy, and he took strong measures to suppress their influence. He also infiltrated the unions, removed leaders, and reorganized many of the shops into the labor confederations that were under his command, primarily the CGT. This became the militant arm of the Peronist machine. It was able to mobilize people and resources to respond against political opponents.[62] As a result, he alienated the more ideologically motivated leftist groups, such as the socialists and communists. They saw Peron as an opportunist who used organized labor as an instrument to promote his personal agenda. In their eyes, he would always be a military man with no understanding of the principles of class struggle.

Peron's confrontational style alienated many powerful groups, and by 1955, the opposition approached the military to launch another coup. With two terms under his belt and no sign of letting up, many people were tired of Peron. His arrogance also allowed him to make silly mistakes. The death of Evita in 1952, as she campaigned for his reelection, was a terrible blow to Peron's image. Scandals about his personal life soon emerged, and his popularity plunged. This led to a series of confrontations with the Catholic Church, which ended in excommunication. The Church initially supported Peron, but his policies had intruded into areas that were considered the Church's exclusive domain, such as education and charity. He legalized divorce and abolished compulsory religious education. All of these events helped turn the tide

---

62 Daniel James, *Resistance and Integration: Peronism and the Argentine Working Class, 1946-1976* (Cambridge: Cambridge University Press, 1988), 9.

against him. In 1955, the military finally deposed Peron and sent him into exile.

The cause of Peron's collapse as a national and political leader is a topic that bewilders many scholars.[63] The unions, military, and political factions that benefited from the Peronist machine did not react to the coup. It was as if they were happy to see him go, as long as he left the machine untouched. Peron clearly left behind a strong institutional framework that would guide the country's corporatist policies for the rest of the century and into the next. Unfortunately, it would not guide it in a way that would optimize the country's resources, welfare, or political stability. In many ways, it would be the main culprit for many of Argentina's woes. Just as Buenos Aires had been the key to controlling the provinces during the early part of the country's history, the Peronist political machine would become the central element in governing Argentina henceforth.

---

63 Celia Szusterman, *Frondizi and the Politics of Developmentalism in Argentina, 1955-62* (London: The Macmillan Press, 1993), 3.

Anarchy and Order

The coup against Peron marked the political return of the landed aristocracy, yet their hold on power was tenuous. The next two and a half decades were marked by political instability that descended into anarchy. Peron's mobilization of the masses was too much to undo, and his changes to the economy were very deep. The oligarchy used several measures to undermine the machinery that Peron put in place. They held a constitutional convention to redo the country's Magna Carta. They outlawed the Peronist Party and persecuted party leaders. Nevertheless, they could not ignore the power that was now at their disposal nor the realities of the global economy, and they ultimately used the Peronist machine to impose social order through the formation of an authoritarian regime.

The leader of the coup was General Eduardo Lonardi, and he titled the uprising the *Revolucion Libertadora* or the Liberating Revolution. The phrase was used to create an image of the country breaking the shackles of Peron's despotism. At the same time, it was meant to be the liberation from the tyranny of the masses and a move toward a more liberal form of economic management.[64] This theme developed during the latter half of the twentieth century. There was a growing desire to liberalize the Argentine economy and return to the glory days of the First World War, but the government would always fall short of the mark. Political necessities prevented it from fully embracing a more liberal form of economic organization until all of the other choices were exhausted.

Lonardi was assisted by other senior members of the high command, particularly General Pedro Aramburu and Admiral Issac Rojas. At first, there was little resistance to the new regime, but as time wore on, the opposition began to mount. The changes that Peron made to Argentine society were almost impossible to reverse. He gave voice to the underclass, a segment of society that had been completely ignored since the founding of the nation. There was dissent in other sectors, as well. For example, parts of the military were still loyal to Peron. The militant elements of the labor unions, particularly the CGT, formed armed militias that became known as the *montoneros*. Although Lonardi promised to call elections as soon as order was established, he seized the Peronist political apparatus to promote his own personal objectives. It was clear that the machine was too much of a temptation to let sit idle. In the absence of any other meaningful institutions, it was the key to controlling Argentina. With the growth of industry, agriculture no longer played such a dominant role. The new key to power in Argentina was the political

---

64 Daniel Rodríguez Lamas, *La Revolución Libertadora* (Buenos Aires: Centro Editor de América Latina, 1985).

apparatus. To that end, Lonardi launched the slogan "Peronism without Peron."[65] Nevertheless, he still had to respond to the interest groups that had backed him in the first place. Therefore, he devalued the currency, which reduced the real income levels of the working class and boosted the profitability of exporters. The measures sparked riots and strikes, and it helped fuel a yearning for the return of the old leader. Wracked by growing social unrest, dissent within elements of the military, and the discovery of terminal cancer, Lonardi was ousted by General Aramburu two months after the coup. Aramburu immediately took stronger measures to dismantle the Peronist movement. He dissolved the party, intervened in the CGT, and arrested senior party leaders. He also commissioned Raul Prebisch, a director of the central bank, to prepare a set of economic reforms to restore the Argentine economy to its former grandeur. Prebisch prepared a study in which he recommended further devaluation of the currency, a reduction in government expenditures, and joining of the IMF. Yet, Prebisch was a strong advocate of import substitution industrialization, and he left an indelible mark on Argentina and the rest of the continent. In 1949, after he was appointed head of the United Nations Economic Commission for Latin America (ECLA), he argued that the only way the region could shake off its historical backwardness was through state-led industrialization.[66] Therefore, the commitment to return to a liberal form of economic management was far from complete.

---

65 David Rock, *Argentina 1516-1987* (Los Angeles: University of California Press, 1987), 134.

66 Celia Szusterman, *Frondizi and the Politics of Developmentalism in Argentina, 1955-62*, (London: The Macmillan Press, 1993), 81.

For the next three years, Aramburu tried to restore political and economic stability, but internal and external conditions were not helping. The persecution of Peronist leaders, the reduction of social benefits, and the devaluation of the currency only served to rehabilitate Peron's image. The socialists were also unable to get rid of the diehard Peronists within the rank and file. A decade of rising wages and improving benefits was too much of a legacy to allow the more ideological leaders to return.[67] Nevertheless, the military junta remained committed to dismantling the movement. Therefore, they called a special election in 1956 to select delegates for a constitutional convention. Unfortunately, a quarter of the ballots were submitted blank, and there was a great deal of dissent among the members. As a result, the only thing the assembly managed to do was to restore the original constitution of 1853. At the same time, the Argentine economy was struggling. The self-imposed isolationism of India and China was starting to bite. Commodity exporters sought alternative markets for their products, and prices remained in the doldrums. As a result, Argentina's balance of payments deteriorated, producing a precipitous decline in international reserves. Moreover, there were important changes taking place on the local industrial landscape. The late 1950s witnessed the rise of the multinational corporation (MNC). Facing high tariff barriers for their products, many manufacturers jumped the wall by opening assembly plants in the developing world. Automobile, electro-domestic, and telecommunications factories were inaugurated in Argentina. Although the new plants allowed the MNCs to hop over the barriers to entry, they still

---

67 Daniel James, *Resistance and Integration: Peronism and the Argentine Working Class, 1946-1976* (Cambridge: Cambridge University Press, 1988), 67.

relied heavily on imported capital equipment, components, and parts. Therefore, the net impact on the country's balance of payments was minimal. These external and internal factors made it difficult for the Argentine economy to pull out of its slump. Facing such a range of insurmountable obstacles, the military hierarchy was not too enthusiastic at remaining at the helm, so they called for new elections in 1958.

The electoral slate was a bit bare this time around. With the Peronist Party outlawed, the Radicals were the only party capable of winning the day. Unfortunately, it was split in two. The UCRP was led by Ricardo Balbin, a lawyer from Buenos Aires who represented the traditional faction of the party. The UCRI was led by Arturo Frondizi, a lawyer from the province of Corrientes. Sensing the immense strength of the Peronist movement, Frondizi realized that the only way he could win the elections was by aligning himself with the former president's followers. Therefore, he took steps to broker an informal alliance with them. The ploy worked, and Frondizi was swept into office, beating Balbin by a huge margin.[68]

The military and members of the landed aristocracy were happy to be rid of Peron, but they were suspicious of Frondizi. He seemed too cozy with them. Sadly, their suspicions turned out to be true. It was not so much that Frondizi was conspiring with the movement, but that he was incapable of satisfying their wishes. His practice of accommodation turned out to be disastrous because the Peronists made higher demands each time he acquiesced. Juan Peron was also drifting back into the limelight. From his refuge in Venezuela, Peron began playing a bigger role in forming public opinion.

---

68 David Rock, *Argentina 1516-1987* (Los Angeles: University of California Press, 1987), 337.

The tensions on the political front were complemented by new economic challenges. Frondizi's policies were aggravating the country's economic woes. His penchant for granting large wage increases and keeping utility rates low converted most of the SOEs into loss-making operations. His preference for import substitution industrialization was also an issue. In an effort to create a domestic industrial base, the government began favoring domestic firms as the main suppliers to the large SOEs. Firms such as Perez Companc and Techint began to gestate as they provided goods and services to the state-owned giants. It was a replay of the provincial operations used to supply the miners of Potosi. Nevertheless, their services were often expensive, and thus were a drain on the government's coffers. Moreover, many of them were fronts for foreign companies. As a result, Argentina's fiscal accounts fell deep into the red. Unable to balance the books, the authorities resorted to printing money, and inflation spiraled out control.

Despite the rhetoric about reverting to a more liberal approach, Argentine policymakers were becoming more heterodox. It was not an issue of ideology; it was a matter of pragmatism. There was immense pressure to accelerate the country's pace of economic development. At the turn of the twentieth century, living standards in Argentina were comparable to Europe, yet the gap was now widening, with Europe pulling ahead. Foolishly, scholars and economists blamed this on the lack of industrialization and not on the declining terms of trade. As a result, the move to heterodoxy was compounding their national woes. Argentina was not the only country to suffer from these mistakes. Brazil, under the leadership of Juscelino Kubitschek, followed a similar path. This was the age of structural functionalism, whereby academics argued that the building of roads, laboratories, and factories would create a sufficient condition for economic development, without any regard to the construction of educational institutions or the strengthening of values and human capital.

Frondizi's hold on power, unfortunately, was coming undone. Although the Radical Party was well established, it had a long legacy of weak administration. Most of the party's presidents were unseated in coups or uprisings. Radical candidates typically ran on platforms of honesty and the need for political reform, but they were often incapable of governing the nation. This weakness provided opportunities for competitors to vie for power and destabilize the country. Yet, the problem was not just with the Radicals. Argentina has an extended lineage of well-intentioned leaders, from Moreno to Castelli to Alem, who were unable to confront entrenched groups and either weaken them or persuade them to their cause. Frondizi was incapable of standing up to the military and Peronist labor unions. Hence, in 1959, he finally switched sides by allying himself with the military and allowing them to suppress the rebellious factions of the Peronist Party.

That same year, the military forced him to oust his Minister of the Economy and appoint Alvaro Alsogaray, an orthodox economist with strong ties to the landed aristocracy. Alsogaray took swift action. With the central bank vaults almost empty, the Argentine government appealed to the IMF for a loan of $328 million. It agreed, but it also imposed several harsh economic measures, including another devaluation of the currency, the downsizing of state-owned companies, and a reduction in government expenditures. The changes hit the economy like a freight train. GDP plunged by 5 percent, and inflation jumped as the effects of the devaluation were transmitted to consumer prices. Given such extreme policies, Peron broke off his support of Frondizi, and the unions took to the streets, thus prompting the military to intensify its repression of all subversive groups.

The 1959 communist uprising in Cuba ignited fears among government leaders that other Latin American countries would follow suit. Armed subversive groups were popping up in Colombia, Brazil, Bolivia, Peru, and Chile. Partially encouraged by Washington, many Latin American governments began implementing programs to infiltrate, repress, and annihilate leftist movements. In 1960, the Argentine military began using torture and murder to root out seditious elements, a process that would gain momentum for the next two decades. However, each action has a reaction, and the subversives began to retaliate.

In the meantime, the Argentine economy was reacting well to Alsogaray's orthodox approach. In 1960, the level of economic activity jumped 8 percent year on year and climbed another 7.1 percent year on year in 1961. The level of industrialization soared with large increases in oil, steel, and automobile output. Foreign investment also jumped as multinationals took advantage of the devalued currency. This short period is often considered the golden age of the Argentine middle class. It was under Frondizi's reign that the economy reached its manufacturing peak.[69] He created tens of thousands of jobs for skilled workers, which produced a powerful economic legacy that would become the foundation of the Radicals' political franchise. Yet, by the eve of 1961, the effects of the new meas-

---

69 Robert Wesson, *U.S. Influence in Latin America in the 1980s* (Stanford: Hoover Institute Press, 1982), 42.

ures were waning. The real exchange began to appreciate as the impact of the devaluation pushed consumer prices higher. Labor unrest was back on the rise. In a desperate move to reduce pressure from the Peronists, Frondizi allowed the party to stand for the gubernatorial elections of 1962. Not surprisingly, the Peronists swept the field. The military immediately insisted that Frondizi annul the elections. When he refused, the troops spilled out of the barracks and deposed him. This pattern repeated itself several times during the next two decades, with devaluations followed by inflationary spikes and social/political unrest.

New presidential elections were called for in 1963. Again, the Peronists were banned from the race, and a new Radical president won the field. This time, Arturo Illia, a country doctor from Cordoba, was elected. With a similar ilk to Frondizi, Illia was doomed from the start. He campaigned on a platform of honesty, democracy, and limiting the influence of foreign corporations, and won with only 25 percent of the votes. The rest of the ballots were split among a field of forty-seven small parties, and there were many blank ballots as well.[70] Furthermore, the Radicals controlled only a third of the seats in Congress. Therefore, there was no way that Illia could stand up to the power of the military or the Peronists. In an effort to thread a course that accommodated both groups, Illia decided to annul the oil exploration and production contracts that were held by foreign companies, in effect nationalizing the entire oil sector and putting it in the hands of YPF. Illia's intent was to make the country energy self-sufficient, in the process appeasing national security

---

70 David Rock, *Argentina 1516-1987* (Los Angeles: University of California Press, 1987), 344.

concerns and creating more jobs. However, YPF lacked the capital, technology, and skilled labor to accomplish such a feat. Therefore, Argentina's oil production plunged, imports soared, and the country's balance of payments went back into the red. By the start of 1966, Illia was on the ropes, and the military was openly preparing for another coup d'état. On June 28, 1966, the armed forces mobilized, and Illia was unceremoniously deposed. He was dumped onto the street and left there, and he walked home.

The leader of the 1966 coup was General Juan Carlos Ongania, a leader of a military faction called the blues. This faction argued for the use of the Peronist machine to impose an authoritarian regime. They argued that this would be the best insurance against the threat of communism. In other words, it was another version of Peronism without Peron.

There was a competing military faction called the reds that advocated a complete dismantling of all Peronist institutions. However, when the unions and Peronists refused to cooperate with Ongania and his blue faction, the military regime shifted into the red camp and resumed its suppressive activities. In 1967, Ongania launched what he termed the Argentine Revolution, a plan to reinvigorate the economy, redistribute wealth, and restore democracy.[71] He appointed Adalbert Kreiger Vasena to lead the effort. Like his predecessors, Kreiger Vasena's first plan of action was to devalue the currency. By now, however, the serial devaluations were creating structural problems, mainly consisting of a persistently high rate of inflation. Knowing the government's penchant for letting the currency go, economic agents anticipated the

---

71 Carlos Ramil Cepeda, *Crisis de una Burguesía Dependiente: Balance Económico de la Revolución Argentina* (Buenos Aires: Edición La Rosa Blindada, 1972), 11.

move by constantly raising prices. The steady rise in inflation fed the atmosphere of social unrest, eventually exploding in 1969.

Cordoba was the epicenter of the uprising. It was the hub of the automobile industry and the location of the oldest and most prestigious university in Argentina. As we saw earlier, the University of Cordoba was established in the earliest days of the empire, and it was founded with the revenues that were generated by the Jesuit Estancias. Even though the university students were mainly from the middle class, they linked up with automobile workers to launch a series of violent protests and strikes. These riots, however, were not unique. All across the planet, from New York, to Paris, to Mexico, young activists were taking to the streets. Yet, the incidents in Cordoba confirmed that the military did not control the country as tightly as it thought. Sensing weakness, other subversive groups increased their activities, including assassinating major political figures, kidnapping businessmen, and detonating bombs. The most destabilizing event was the kidnapping and murder of former dictator Aramburu, and it was clear that darkness was descending upon Argentina.

The presidential mantle again cycled through several more generals, but it seemed that the only way order could be restored was by allowing Peron to return. At the end of 1972, Peron was permitted to visit for the first time since he was ousted, and he was received with a hero's welcome. The military regime called for a presidential election in early 1973, but Peron was not allowed to run. Instead, Hector Campora ran as an open proxy in his place. He easily won the election, and one of his first acts was to release imprisoned guerillas and political activists. He also allowed Peron to return permanently.

Upon his arrival at Ezeiza, the international airport on the outskirts of Buenos Aires, Peron was greeted by half a million supporters—including the militant factions of the labor unions and the *montoneros*. Both groups were armed, and fighting soon broke out among them. Hundreds of people died in the mayhem. This was the first sign that something was amiss. Instead of stabilizing the political environment, Peron's return only added to the instability. Lonardi's aim of relying on Peronism without Peron had become a reality. The movement was now bigger than the leader, and he could do little to control it. Nevertheless, the die was cast. Campora resigned upon Peron's arrival, and new elections were called for September 1973. Not surprisingly, Peron was swept back into power.

Peron's return to office coincided with turmoil in the international markets. The Arab-Israeli War led to an embargo by the major oil producers of the Middle East, which triggered a spike in prices. The geometric rise in oil pushed the global economy into recession and waylaid most of the Latin American economies. Although Argentina struggled to become self-sufficient in energy production through its promotion of YPF, it was still highly dependent on imports. Therefore, the country soon found itself in more difficulties, as higher energy prices pushed up the inflation rate and the country's balance of payments deteriorated. Peron sought to stabilize the economy, but he needed to consolidate his base by purging the most subversive elements of his movement. In a rally in front of the Casa Rosada, Peron publically ejected the *montoneros* from the square and out of the party. The fragmentation of the

Peronist movement added to the perception that the country was in a state of anarchy. Unfortunately, less than a year after his reelection, Peron died suddenly in July of 1974, ending the country's last hope of order being restored.

One of Argentina's political flaws is its failure to establish independent institutions. Unlike other countries, which enjoy independent branches of government, Argentina's disputes have been settled in an open struggle for the control of the political apparatus. During the early part of the nation's history, this meant the control of the customs house. Later, it meant the control of the Peronist machine. Nevertheless, it is the same thing. The customs house was the main source of economic power, and it was physically located in Buenos Aires. The Peronist machine was the mass of urban poor who provided the electoral votes to govern the country. They resided in the outskirts of the city. Therefore, whoever controlled Buenos Aires dominated Argentina.

It's true that Argentina has a long list of well-established political parties that represented different factions at different times in the nation's history. The Unitarians represented Buenos Aires. The Federalists represented the provinces. The Radicals represented the middle class, and the Peronists represented the lumpenproletariat. In addition, there were socialists, communists, and right-wing parties. Still, the rank and file tended to be more loyal to the party leadership rather than to their constituencies. This meant that the political institutions were designed to be machines of political patronage. One of the reasons for this characteristic was the persistent use of electoral lists, whereby people voted for a roll of party candidates rather than a direct representative. Therefore, there was no accountability for individual actions. There was just loyalty to the senior politician who decided on the composition of the list. Argentina has also had a long legacy of electoral fraud, whereby the authorities have manipulated electoral results and defined the outcomes. Given that Argentina was undergoing so much turmoil during the 1960s and 1970s due to the structural changes in the global economy and domestic industry, it did not have the proper political channels to articulate the needs of the country's various interest groups adequately. Hence, the only other way to effect change was through violence.

Unfortunately, the death of Peron was a powerful blow that left the country rudderless. The new problem was his successor. In an attempt to boost his public standing, Peron selected his third wife, Isabella, as his running mate. His intent was to resurrect the image of Evita. However, the vice president suddenly found herself as president. Although very pretty, the former cabaret hostess did not have the charm, charisma, and political acumen of Evita. She also lacked the knowledge and skills to run the country effectively. Eventually, she came under the spell of José Lopez Rega, a Rasputin type of individual who became the puppeteer behind the regime.

Prior to Peron's death, the party was fragmenting. In addition to the *montoneros*, other factions were breaking away. As the movement crumbled into smaller components, the competing factions descended into virtual civil war. There were open acts of violence and civil disobedience throughout the country. Isabella slowly allowed the military to intensify their counter-subversive operations, opening up detention camps and torture centers. Hundreds of people were "disappeared" as the military and police cast their net farther afield to take

in anyone remotely associated to or considered to have connections with the political left. Abetted by the United States,
and with similar programs underway in other Latin American
countries, the Argentine government went after students, pro-
fessors, clerics, and union leaders. Argentines began fleeing
the country as the repression increased. By March of 1976,
the country was in the midst of economic and social chaos,
and the military was forced to step in.

The next six years marked the darkest chapter in Argentine history. Known as the Dirty War, the military regime pulled
out the stops in trying to suppress all elements of the Peronist
movement. Led by General Jorge Videla, Argentina became
a fully militarized authoritarian state. Due process of law was
thrown to the wind, and military patrols carried out arbitrary
executions. The country had returned to the lawlessness of
the postindependence days when bands of gauchos terrorized the countryside. Although the military went to great effort
to eradicate the political and social components of the Peronist movement, they did not dismantle its economic base.
On the contrary, they used the deluge of global liquidity to
bolster the country's industrial foundation.

On one hand, the oil crisis of the early 1970s was a powerful blow to the developed world, but on the other hand,
it was a massive redistribution of wealth into oil-producing
countries. Faced with the windfall of higher oil revenues, the
governments of these countries deposited their capital into
the large central banks. Much of the funds found their way
into the US property market, but they also made their way
into the developing world. Investment bankers were seen
bouncing through the financial centers of Latin America ped-
dling syndicated loans. The Argentine military junta took

advantage of the liquidity by borrowing billions of dollars to build shipyards, munitions factories, and technology laboratories. Signing on major multinational firms such as IBM and Siemens, the Argentine military tried to accelerate the country's pace of development by creating rival technological formats in sectors such as computing and telecommunications. The multinationals loved it. They often supplied outdated equipment and technology while charging princely sums for their services. The military junta also imposed high tariff barriers to protect many of the multinationals that were already operating in Argentina, providing protection for industries such as automobiles and steel.

The heavy use of protectionism gave these firms the monopolistic freedom to provide goods and services at the highest possible prices with no retribution. The result was a steady decline in the quality of Argentine manufactures, a loss of competitiveness, and a gradual decline in per capita income.

With discontent spreading, the military used desperate ploys to placate the masses. It fixed the World Cup match against Peru in 1978, and in a last act of desperation, it embarked on an ill-fated attempt to regain control of the Malvinas in 1982. Facing the iron will of Prime Minister Margaret Thatcher, the Argentine high command never imagined that the British would risk their fleet to recover a handful of windswept islands in the South Atlantic. Even though the Argentine military fought valiantly, particularly the air force, the Argentine invasion force was soundly defeated. As a result, the military's attempt to restore order in the aftermath of almost three decades of political, social, and economic instability ended in defeat.

The protagonists of this era were the various political parties, military officers, and labor factions that dominated Argentina between 1955 and 1982, but the two main players were the agricultural sector and the Peronist political machine. Both institutions were in flux. The declining role of agriculture fed the atmosphere of anarchy as one of the pillars of the economy lost its hegemonic power. The steady decline in commodity prices after the Second World War undermined Argentina's economy. This vacuum created an opportunity for other actors, such as the military, labor unions, and industrialists, to compete for control. The only group that was able to do so was the Peronist Party. Rooted in the greater Buenos Aires area, it controlled the electoral votes that would decide the nation's leadership. Peronism was also an economic system that used the country's industrialization program to redistribute income, pay tribute, and obtain patronage. The struggle for the control of the Peronist machine and the decline of the agricultural sector plunged the country into a prolonged period of instability, which ended in civil war and an ignoble defeat at the hands of the British. Exhausted, the country started making a slow turn toward liberalism as the only way to optimize its potential.

Liberalism Run Amuck

The renaissance of the liberal movement was born out of the ashes of the Second World War. The conflict polarized the planet. On one pole, Russia and China advocated communism. On the other pole, the United States championed free market policies. In the middle, a vast array of mixed approaches used free-market techniques along with socialist instruments. The attempt to impose a homogeneous system on the entire world triggered the Cold War and four decades of proxy conflicts. Despite the intensity of the competition, there was still a general shift toward leftist ideals. Most of Europe remained capitalist while embracing policies that provided high levels of social benefits in return for equally high levels of taxation. Labor unions were allowed to play an important role in making policy decisions, and there was a proliferation of SOEs. Even the United States took a turn to the left. In the aftermath of the Great Depression, President Franklin Delano Roosevelt introduced the New Deal, which allowed the government to play a larger role in the allocation of resources. Keynesianism was the dominant economic theory of the postwar period, and there was widespread use of centralized planning. Yet, in the distant outpost of Chicago, a new economic movement was taking root during the early 1970s.

There were clear limits with centrally directed economic programs. It was impossible to take into account all contingencies, scenarios, and random events. This led to the misallocation of resources, thus producing famines and millions of deaths. The nationalization of assets and the collectivization of farms deprecated the individual and stymied innovation. Authors such as Ayn Rand railed against the insanity of the approach. Eventually, the ideas moved into the academic realm, with theorists examining the role of the individual in the formation of economic decision-making. Economists such as Robert Coase, Gary Becker, and Milton Friedman formed a school of thought that rejected the principles of central planning. Instead, they focused on the incentives and preferences that motivated individual behavior. This was a new twist on the neoclassical approach that had been pioneered by Marx and Engels a century earlier. Like the Marxists, the Chicago School recognized the primacy of the business cycle. Instead of using collective action and state ownership to smooth the amplitudes of the oscillations, they preferred to use other methods to shape aggregate decisions. Keynesians advocated the use of fiscal policy, but the Chicago School, led by Friedman, argued for the use of monetary policy. Furthermore, they believed that by reducing the role of the state, societies would allocate resources in the most efficient way—thus boosting income levels. Known as neoliberalism, the concepts were spread throughout the world by the graduates of the University of Chicago. Many of them were upper middle-class students who went abroad and became virtual acolytes of this new religion.

The most acute example occurred in Chile, where recent graduates infiltrated the military government of Augusto Pinochet and became aptly known as the Chicago Boys. Their free-market policies transformed the Chilean economy and sent it along a bumpy path toward greater prosperity. In the mid-1970s, the Chicago School played an important role in shaping Margret Thatcher's economic proposals. In Argentina, it would be some time before neoliberalism would become the dominant framework, but there were already serious forays in that direction, particularly by Economy Ministers Alvaro Alsogaray and Adalbert Kreiger Vasena. Yet, there remained a statist bent to the policy mix. The military's control of the economic and labor apparatus dovetailed nicely with its authoritarian approach.[72] Therefore, the promise to move to a more liberal economic framework would take some time before manifesting itself fully.

The anarchy that followed the death of Peron signaled the need to embark in a new economic direction. In 1976, General Videla appointed Cambridge-educated economist José Alfredo Martinez de Hoz as Minister of the Economy. Because Martinez de Hoz hailed from one of the oldest families in Argentina, he was considered the direct representative of the landed aristocracy. The new minister took stark measures to stabilize the economy, regain competitiveness, and restore growth. The CGT was abolished, wages were frozen,

---

72 Philippe C. Schmitter and Gerhard Lehmbruch, *Trends towards corporatist intermediation* (London: Sage Publications, 1979).

and the currency devalued. With strong connections to international banks and the IMF, Martinez de Hoz put together a plan that would stimulate the private sector by attracting billions of dollars in foreign investment. In many ways, it was an extension of the Krieger Vasena plan, but more ideological and extreme in its implementation. Yet, Martinez de Hoz was never fully able to embrace the neoliberal model, primarily because he was unable to privatize the SOEs and rein in fiscal spending. Under his watch, the state-owned entities actually grew in size. The reason for the lack of privatization was that most of the companies were run by the military, and they were virtual cash cows for the high command.

Pampered by lavish compensation schemes and luxurious benefits, the generals did not want to divest their companies. However, the SOEs were unprofitable, and saddled the government with huge losses. Another problem was a major rearmament initiative. Like boys with toys, the return of the military allowed the top brass to embark on an extensive buying spree. Fighters, missiles, and warships were acquired. Expensive training programs were secured. In 1977, a pending arbitration process by Britain over the demarcation of the border between Chile and Argentina was finally concluded, resulting in a favorable decision for Chile. At stake was the sovereignty of three islands in the Beagle Channel. Not only was the region strategically important as one of the main conduits of global trade; it was brimming with natural resources—including oil. Chile's attempt to act upon the ruling led to a sharp rebuke by the military junta in Buenos Aires, and the two countries almost went to war.

The losses generated by the rearmament program and the SOEs led to a significant widening of the fiscal deficit. With the situation spiraling out of control, Martinez de Hoz resorted to a toxic mix of monetary expansion and the opening of the capital account. The result was a spike in the inflation rate, pressure on the peso, and a large increase in foreign debt. With consumer prices rising north of 175 percent per year, Martinez de Hoz introduced a crawling peg system, called La Tablita, which provided a steady devaluation of the currency. This was supposed to act as a nominal anchor to stabilize consumer prices. The problem was that it served as a mechanism to build in the expectations of future devaluations, thus intensifying the inflationary pressures. Moreover, the government's inability to reduce the fiscal deficit only added to the momentum. Given that the inflation rate was higher than the pace of devaluation, the currency appreciated dramatically in real terms. Argentine firms lost competitiveness, and the government was forced to rely more on international capital to cover its external shortfall. Additional measures were introduced in 1979 to liberate the current and capital accounts, thus allowing firms to access the international markets to meet their financing needs. The proliferation of small banks that obtained funding abroad was a virtual replay of the policies that plagued President Juarez Celman during 1890.

Argentina's foreign obligations tripled between 1979 and the end of Videla's government in March 1981, reaching $25.3 billion.[73] The end of the regime coincided with the exit of Martinez de Hoz. By the next year, the country was embroiled in the disastrous Malvinas War. Soon after the defeat in the South Atlantic, mass graves of political prisoners were discovered in the Province of Buenos Aires.

---

73 David Rock, *Argentina 1516-1987* (Los Angeles: University of California Press, 1987), 373-374.

Likewise, the weekly protest marches by the mothers of the disappeared gained worldwide recognition. It was clear that the support, credibility, and legitimacy of the military regime were gone. Elections were called for October 1982, and the Radicals fielded a new champion, Raul Alfonsin. A lawyer from the Province of Buenos Aires, he rose steadily through the ranks of the Radical Party. He was a vocal critic of the war, and lent his services to defend the political prisoners of the military regime. As happened in the past, the Radicals promised to eradicate the country's woes. Yet, they were no match for the entrenched groups. The Peronists were weakened during the dictatorship, but the movement was never destroyed. Hence, the Peronist Party presented a presidential candidate, Italo Luder, for the elections, and he won a respectable 40 percent of the vote, thus allowing the party to reintegrate itself with the political process. However, changes were taking place abroad that would have powerful consequences at home.

In addition to the effects of the oil embargo of the 1970s, the United States experienced a period of fiscal mismanagement and high inflation. The combination of the Space Race, the Vietnam War, and Lyndon Johnson's Great Society widened the deficit and sent consumer prices soaring. Between 1972 and 1974, inflation rose to over 12 percent as higher energy prices delivered powerful shockwaves throughout the economy. Unfortunately, Washington's efforts to stabilize the situation were ineffective. The Nixon administration, for example, tried a strange variety of heterodox policies to tame inflation, including price controls and publicity campaigns. Not surprisingly, they were to no avail, and inflation continued to climb higher. In April 1980, the annualized increase in consumer prices reached almost 15 percent. Something drastic had to be done. In 1982, the chairman of the Federal Reserve, Paul Volcker, took action. Taking a cue from the theoretical advances that were taking shape at the University of Chicago, Volcker clamped down on monetary policy by raising interest rates to 16 percent. A decade of easy money came to a sudden stop. Home prices in the United States collapsed as domestic demand contracted and the availability of new loans evaporated. Inflation slowed, but the tightening of monetary policy pushed the US economy into a recession. With the United States representing almost a third of global output, the North American downturn spread abroad quickly.

The changes on the US monetary front aggravated the crisis for the hapless Argentines. The country's banks were facing serious liquidity problems even before the Fed's move. The Malvinas War forced British banks to freeze Argentine assets, removing a major source of liquidity. They also stopped participating in all syndicated loans for Argentina. To make matters worse, four months after the invasion of the South Atlantic islands, Mexican Finance Minister Jesus Silva Herzog called the Federal Reserve Bank of New York to declare a moratorium on external debt payments. International banks immediately halted all syndicated lending, eliminating the ability of the country to roll over its mountain of debt. The interest on the syndicated loans floated according to a benchmark rate. Therefore, as interest rates soared, due to the tightening of US monetary policy, so did the rates on the loans. By 1985, the increase in interest payments was $600 million per year, and the Argentine government was going into arrears. The government was not yet in a full-fledged default, but it was holding on by a thread. Washington tried to assuage the situation through the Baker Plan. Under the auspices of the program, the IMF provided liquidity to developing countries as long as they followed its macroeconomic guidelines and used the funds to meet external obligations.

These external and internal conditions created a perfect storm for the new, democratically elected government. The economy was in shambles. The military was defeated and discredited. At the same time, Argentine society was trying to come to grips with the human rights violations perpetrated by the military regime. For its first eighteen months in office, the Alfonsin administration focused on social issues. Yet, inflation continued to be a problem. In 1984, the monthly inflation rate reached 20 percent. Alfonsin's Minister of the Economy, Bernardo Grinspun, struggled to stabilize the situation, but was unsuccessful. One of the main culprits was the indexation caused by La Tablita. It induced an inflationary momentum that was difficult to break. Therefore, in June 1985, the government launched the Austral Plan. Like previous stabilization plans, it sought to rein in the fiscal deficit. However, it had several new features that distinguished it from previous initiatives. The plan introduced a new currency unit called the austral. The government promised not to finance the fiscal shortfall through monetary expansion, and it vowed to reduce the losses of SOEs. The architect of the Austral Plan was Juan Sourrouille, who was assisted by a league of top-rated economists, such as Ricardo Lopez Murphy (a graduate of the University of Chicago) and José Luis Machinea.

The Austral Plan attended the two main problems that were fueling the runaway inflation rate. The new currency unit broke the psychological expectations of higher price adjustments. The government also prevented the central bank from financing the fiscal gap through monetary expansion. Consumer prices suddenly stabilized, and the monthly inflation rate dropped to 2 to 3 percent.[74] Not surprisingly, the plan was hugely popular, and it allowed the Radicals to sweep the midterm elections in October 1985. However, it did not really take care of the core fiscal problem. Sourrouille promised to keep the employment level high at state-owned companies. Therefore, they continued to post huge losses. These shortfalls were exacerbated by the price controls that froze the companies' revenues but left them exposed to increases in costs. By the end of 1985, the fiscal deficit was 4.5 percent of GDP. Unable to finance the gap through monetary emissions, the government turned to the external market. The problem was that the sovereign was already in arrears. Therefore, small banks and brokers began to borrow domestically and abroad to finance the public sector.

For the next two years, the government increased its borrowing program. Much of it was from local households and businesses that took advantage of the high nominal interest rates. In 1987, the government began relaxing price controls, only to see the inflation rate explode. At the same time, the Alfonsin administration was facing pressure from the labor unions. In an effort to declaw the Peronist movement, Alfonsin introduced a set of reforms that would allow free and open elections for leadership positions. The elections would be administered and supervised by government officials. The idea was to break the party's stranglehold on the union's leadership and remove one of the most powerful tools at its disposal.

Not surprisingly, the labor unions reacted violently. They launched a series of devastating national strikes, culminating

---

74 Manuel Solanet, *La hiperinflación del 89* (Buenos Aires: Lumiere, 2006), 61.

in eight labor stoppages in 1987. It almost broke the back of the Alfonsin government. Likewise, the military was agitating. The ongoing investigations and trials of military officers reached a breaking point by the start of 1988. Army groups in Cordoba and Buenos Aires began to mutiny, led by officers who had fought valiantly in the war against Britain. The uprisings were put down peacefully, but it was clear that the Radicals were on the ropes.

The economic instability produced by high inflation was tearing the social fabric apart. Therefore, they decided to introduce another stabilization program. Known as the Spring Plan, it was similar to the Austral Plan, except it did not introduce a new currency unit. There was also a bigger effort to balance the fiscal accounts by freezing wages and imposing price controls. Nevertheless, it was not enough, and the government found itself cornered. Squeezed by the need to stabilize consumer prices while facing an insurmountable pile of debt, it decided to forego its external obligations. Therefore, in April 1988, Argentina formally declared a moratorium on its debt payments, throwing the country into default on an external debt stock of $62 billion.[75]

To make matters worse, the presidential elections were scheduled for May 1989, and a great deal of uncertainty was in the air. The electoral slate consisted of three candidates. The Radicals were led by Eduardo Angeloz, the Governor of Cordoba. Former Economy Minister Alvaro Alsogaray was running under the conservative banner of the Union for the Democratic Center (UCeDe), and the Peronist candidate was Carlos Menem, the flamboyant Governor of La Rioja. Unfor-

---

75 Eugenio Andrea Bruno, *El Default y la Reestructacion de la Deuda* (Buenos Aires: Nueva Mayoría, 2004), 123.

tunately, the polls showed Menem in the lead. A flagrant populist, Menem represented the worst of the Peronist stereotype. As the day approached and Menem took the field, the currency plunged, pushing the country into hyperinflation. Everyone rounded on Sourrouille and blamed the Spring Plan for the country's runaway inflation rate. Even Angeloz, the Radical candidate, called for his resignation—thus forcing him to take a bow. However, Sourrouille's departure only heightened the sense of panic. In May, there were lootings of supermarkets and widespread social unrest. Many people thought that the military would be called in to establish law and order. Therefore, President Alfonsin tendered his resignation early and allowed Menem to take over three months ahead of time.

As people abandoned the austral in order to hoard dollars, the value of the currency plunged. Consumer prices soared 3,079 percent year on year in 1989. All valuations lost their significance. Restaurants refused to put prices on their menus, using reference tables that were updated several times a day. With confidence lost, people resorted to dollars as their only store of value. It was clear that drastic measures were needed. Menem turned to the Argentine corporate sector and appointed Miguel Angel Roig, a senior executive of the agricultural giant Bunge & Born, as minister of the economy. The new minister quickly introduced a package of measures known as Plan BB (for Bunge & Born). This plan included the introduction of a new currency unit, a widespread privatization program, and the independence of the central bank. Unfortunately, Roig suffered a fatal heart attack five days after taking office, and the country plunged into chaos. Menem immediately appointed another Bunge &

Born executive, Nestor Rapanelli, to succeed him. Rapanelli announced several legislative packages. The first one was the Reform of the State, which finally allowed the Argentine government to rid itself of the lumbering SOEs that were the main source of the fiscal hole. It allowed the executive branch to intervene, restructure, and privatize all state companies. He also introduced the Emergency Economic Law, which allowed the government to implement the necessary reforms to confront the ongoing crisis.[76] Lastly, Rapanelli secured funding through the IMF Standby Credit Facility, which allowed it to keep servicing some of its external obligations. Nevertheless, domestic debt levels had reached unmanageable proportions, and servicing it had become another driver of the country's persistent hyperinflation.

By the end of 1989, Rapanelli was out. He was replaced by Erman Gonzalez. Although Gonzalez had a brief stint as the Economy Minister, he played an important role in reprofiling the country's debt load. The explosive increase in domestic obligations was choking the economy. Therefore, the government launched a compulsory exchange that converted deposits and local debt into long-term foreign-denominated instruments. The forced exchange, known as Bonex, drained liquidity and pushed the economy into a deeper recession, but it stabilized the country's domestic debt levels. In February 1991, Gonzalez was replaced by Domingo Cavallo, a Harvard-educated economist who started his academic career at the University of Cordoba. The appointment of Cavallo marked the point when Argentina fully embraced liberalism, and the country became the poster child of the international

---

76 Ana Margheritis, *Ajuste y Reforma En Argentina (1989-1995)* (Buenos Aires: Nuevohacer, 1999), 53.

financial community. Cavallo's arrival coincided with a sea change on the international stage. In 1991, the Soviet Union dissolved, ending more than seven decades of Communist rule. At the same time, a triumphant United States-led coalition vanquished the formidable military forces of Saddam Hussein in the Gulf War. These two events marked the collapse of communism and the ascendency of free market capitalism.

For the next decade, Argentina moved into the vanguard of the transformation process by becoming the paradigm of liberalism. The new Argentine government changed its position in regards to the United States. Instead of pursuing an antagonistic approach toward Washington, Menem moved closer. For the next decade, the government embraced the free-market policies espoused by the Washington Consensus. Menem dispatched troops to bolster US military adventures, and the country entered into a "carnal relationship" with North America.[77]

Roig announced the introduction of a new currency unit at the start of President Menem's term, but it was not done until Cavallo took over. The new currency system became known as the Convertibility Plan, and it was based around a currency board. Similar to what was done by President Juarez Celman, the central bank limited its monetary issues to the level of international reserves. Given that the new peso was pegged to the dollar, the central bank was restricted in its emissions. All issuance needed to be backed by an equal amount of dollars. In other words, all discretion was taken out of monetary policymaking, and it was now a rule-based system. In reality,

---

77 Eduardo Conesa, *Que Pasa en la Economía Argentina* (Buenos Aires: Ediciones Macchi, 2000), 67.

the move to the Convertibility Plan was very pragmatic. The episode of hyperinflation had all but dollarized the economy. Therefore, the greenback was the primary instrument for transactions. The introduction of a currency unit that was pegged to the dollar was the only way of regaining access to a locally denominated money supply.

In order to ensure the efficacy of the new monetary system, the government legislated the independence of the central bank, thus freeing it from the chains of the political process. The next measure was the acceleration of the privatization program. Although the government vowed for decades to shed its state-owned companies, there was a genuine commitment to divest them as soon as possible. To begin with, the Peronists were at the helm, and they could manage the sale. This was the reason they always blocked the attempts by Alfonsin to divest them. Using the powers authorized by the Reform of the State, the government introduced a process whereby local industrialists and the unions played an important role in the sale and management of the new firms, thus allowing the party to feed its patronizing machine. As a result, the entire range of SOEs was sold off. The railroads, telephone and gas companies, and even YPF, the state-owned oil giant, were put on the block. Indeed, Argentina undertook the most extensive privatization program in its history. It even went further than Chile, which never managed to sell off ENAP, its national oil company.

Argentina sold more than sixty SOEs generating more than $45 billion in revenues.[78] Much of the initial revenues were in the form of debt-to-equity swaps, which significantly lowered

---

78 World Bank, "Progress in Privatization in Developing Countries," *Global Development Finance* (Washington: World Bank, 2001): 186.

the price for the investors making the acquisition. Not surprisingly, the international financial community was extremely enthusiastic about the privatization program. The sale of state assets in other countries, such as Mexico and Chile, were generating huge fees for the banks leading the transactions. The newly privatized firms needed to raise capital in the form of shares or bonds to modernize their machinery, equipment, and capital stock, thus generating additional fees. Multinational firms were also anxious to participate in the deals. Facing mature markets at home, access to the developing world offered them opportunities to deploy techniques and technology to boost revenues while enjoying favorable operating conditions for a number of years. Not surprisingly, a powerful lobby of western bankers and industrialists leaned heavily on the multilateral lending agencies, such as the IMF, World Bank, and Inter-American Development Bank (IADB) to encourage developing countries to pursue privatization programs—thus becoming a major platform of the Washington Consensus.

In addition to the sale of state assets, Cavallo privatized the national pension system, thus creating a network of privately owned pension funds (AFJPs). Like most countries around the world, Argentina's pension system was set up on a pay-as-you-go basis. This meant that current contributions to the pension system were used to pay current obligations. It was in contrast to a fully funded system, as was used in Chile, whereby workers contributed to their own retirement plans. This private system encouraged savings and created a pool of domestic capital that could be used for national development, thus reducing its dependence on the capital markets.

The sale of state assets trimmed the fiscal deficit. Nevertheless, government revenues were still low due to high levels of tax evasion. Therefore, Cavallo took steps to widen the tax base. He eliminated many of the exemptions to taxes and beefed up the government's tax collection efforts by expanding the operations of the national tax collection agency (AFIP).

Next, he pivoted his attention to the external side of the equation. He began with the liberation of the trade accounts. Observing the persistent weakness in the commodity markets, he decided to boost the export of manufactured goods. However, he knew that the developed world was not interested in importing Argentine manufactured products. They lacked the technology and quality to be of interest abroad. Fortunately, Argentina was adjacent to Brazil, one of the largest and most inefficient economies in the world, which meant that Argentine firms would enjoy a considerable competitive advantage. To that end, the government signed the Treaty of Asuncion. The new customs union, known as Mercosur, allowed Argentina to integrate itself with Brazil, Uruguay, and Paraguay. Particularly, it gave Argentine automobile and auto parts producers greater access to the burgeoning Brazilian market.

Still, Argentina needed access to the international capital markets to modernize its infrastructure and industry. Furthermore, the improvement in fiscal receipts was not enough to cover all of the government's financing needs. By the time Cavallo became the minister of the economy, the Argentine sovereign had been shut out of the international capital markets for almost a decade. The bond issues that were completed at the end of Alfonsin's term were done by local issuers, mainly banks. Unfortunately, most of the emerging world was in a similar situation. The debt crisis that started in Mexico spread to more than two dozen countries. At first, the problem was considered a liquidity crisis, and it was treated as such by the Baker Plan. However, the prolongation of the crisis put governments deep into arrears because they were forced to pay fines and interest on past due interest. In other words, the liquidity crisis evolved into a solvency crisis as governments faced burgeoning debt loads that were insurmountable. Hence, any restructuring would require a reduction in principal.

The debt crisis of the 1980s should have been addressed quickly, but the problems in the emerging world were only part of the troubles faced by the large central banks. The liquidity boom of the 1970s produced a housing bubble in the United States that imploded with the hike in interest rates. Faced with the compounded woes of high mortgage delinquencies and the debt crisis, many US banks found themselves technically insolvent. To prevent a national banking crisis, the Federal Reserve modified its accounting rules to allow local institutions to carry their emerging market portfolios at historical values instead of at current valuations. Foreign banks, however, were not as exposed to the US mortgage market. Therefore, they decided to write down the value of their emerging market loans. The variance between the two groups was one of the main reasons the debt crisis lasted so long, and the 1980s became known as the Lost Decade for much of the developing world.

The fact that most of the sovereign lending of the 1970s was in the form of syndicated loans meant that all of the members of the syndicate had to be in agreement in order to proceed with any restructuring process. The central banks that organized the loans were based in the United States, Europe, and Japan. The Europeans and Japanese were anxious to get on with the process. They had already written down the value of their investments, and a resolution to the crisis would most likely result in capital gains. Hence, they were open to the idea of granting the debtors a reduction in principal. The American banks, which had been carrying the value of the loans at historical levels, would most likely face capital losses in any restructuring scenario. Therefore, they were in no hurry to provide any reduction in principal—at least until they beefed up their balance sheets.

The impasse was solved by Treasury Undersecretary David Mulford. His idea was to convert the loans into bonds that could be traded unencumbered in the secondary market. Creditors would be allowed to choose from a menu of options. The first option would be par bonds. Creditors would exchange their loans for bonds that carried the same face value of the loans, but they would receive a below-market coupon payment. The second option would be discount bonds. Creditors would receive bonds with a significant reduction in principal, but with an above-market coupon payment. On a Net Present Value (NPV) basis, both instruments were the same. For those banks unwilling to accept a reduction in principal or a below-market rate, they would be given a New Money option that allowed them to pay in more capital and receive par bonds with above-market coupons. In order to qualify for the program, the governments had to agree to an IMF Standby Facility, which mainly consisted of the reforms outlined in the Washington Consensus.

In order to qualify for the program, debtor countries had to clean up their arrears and buy zero-coupon Treasuries that would be used as collateral for the restructured debt instruments. Given the toxicity of the emerging world, Mulford thought that the only way investors would buy the new bonds was if they were backed by high-quality guarantees. One thing was clear: the official sector wanted to move these loans off the banks' balance sheets and make sure that they never endangered the global financial system.

Mexico was the first country to enter the Brady Plan in 1989, followed by Venezuela in 1990. However, Argentina was unable to accumulate the funds needed to pay down its arrears.[79] The dictates of the Convertibility Plan forced it to husband its hard currency resources. Yet the attitude of the creditor banks was starting to change. Brady bonds were generating huge fees when they began to trade. The rehabilitation of the countries was also making them available to other transactions, such as the issuance of new sovereign and corporate bonds as well as equity issues. Privatizations and M & A transactions were converting emerging market divisions into huge profit centers. Up to this point, they had been obscure backwaters where banks used junior employees to recoup loan losses. Now, these departments were generating billions of dollars in profits as the markets came back to life. Suddenly, there was a need for bankers and specialists with any form of experience and language skills from the developing world. People with Peace Corps experience and even Latin American janitors were put on trading desks. Therefore, it was no surprise that the banks accommodated the countries that were struggling to meet the conditions of the Brady Plan. Instead of cleaning up its arrears, Argentina

---

79 Arnaldo Bocco, *Privatizaciones: Restructuración del Estado y de la Sociedad* (Buenos Aires: Ediciones Letra Buena, 1991), 213.

was allowed to refinance them with new instruments called FRBs. Brazil was allowed to apply a haircut to its arrears and even finance its acquisition of the Treasuries that would collateralize the new par and discount bonds. Wall Street was now in love with the developing world, and it would be the hottest destination for the next two decades.

The siren song of liberalism was sweet for Argentina. Like the Austral Plan, the introduction of the new currency broke the psychological momentum that had kept the country in hyperinflation. The strict rules of the Convertibility Plan also gave people a great deal of confidence that the central bank would not expand the money supply and debase the currency. Moreover, the wholesale privatization program slimmed down the public sector, greatly reducing the fiscal deficit. Last of all, the restructuring of the external debt allowed the country to regain access to the international capital markets, bringing in a deluge of new investment. As a result, the Argentine economy went into overdrive. The decline in the inflation rate increased real wages, thus raising the level of prosperity—particularly for the lower classes. There was also renewed access to credit. Banks raised money on the international capital markets and recycled it domestically, allowing households to buy new cars and homes, and take vacations. Argentina, which until the 1990s was a virtual museum of postwar industrial design, was transforming itself into a hub of modernity, with a network of high-speed fiber optic cables girding Buenos Aires to the latest cellular technology.

Yet, trouble was brewing below the surface. Capital was flowing in, but cracks were starting to appear. The privatization programs allowed the new owners of the companies to downsize their operations. As a result, the unemployment rate rose. Prior to the start of the privatization programs, Argentina's unemployment rate was in the single digits, and by the mid-1990s, it was more than 15 percent.[80] Not surprisingly, public opinion turned against the reforms.[81] There were also problems on the external side. Commodity prices remained in the doldrums. At the same time, the US dollar was remarkably strong. Steps to improve the fiscal accounts and a tech-driven economic recovery allowed the US currency to strengthen. Given that the Argentine currency was pegged to the dollar, the peso appreciated in real terms. Likewise, Argentina's inflation was low, but the residual momentum from the period of hyperinflation was another factor that allowed the real exchange rate to rise, thus putting pressure on the current account.

Cavallo dismissed the mounting concerns, arguing that the current account shortfall was a good thing since it was a byproduct of the large capital inflows. Moreover, many other countries in the region were taking notice of what was happening in Argentina. Brazil, Venezuela, Peru, and Ecuador followed suit by putting their SOEs on the block and embarking on major structural reforms. Therefore, the multilateral lending agencies were keen to make sure that the Argentine ship remained afloat as a shining example for all to see.

In 1993, Argentina's current account deficit was $7.3 billion, but the next year it was $9.3 billion. This represented a shortfall of 3.3 percent of GDP. Much of the capital that was being used to cover the external gap was in the form

---

80 Ana Margheritis, *Ajuste y Reforma En Argentina (1989-1995)* (Buenos Aires: Nuevohacer, 1999), 65.

81 Rosendo Fraga, *Contexto Político y Privatizaciones en la Argentina* (Buenos Aires: Centro de Estudios Union Para la Nueva Mayoría, 1994), 6.

of portfolio investment, and it could exit easily if the situation changed. In February 1994, Alan Greenspan, the chairman of the board of the Federal Reserve, started an unexpected tightening of US monetary policy, which triggered an outflow of funds from the emerging world. It was a replay of what occurred in 1982 when Volcker hiked US rates. Most of the emerging world was at risk because many countries had pegged their currencies to the dollar in an effort to stabilize their economies. The result was disastrous. The canary in the coalmine was Mexico. As Mexico entered the final stages of its presidential race in 1994, the government ran out of international reserves. Mexico was forced to devalue its currency. In a replay of the 1982 debt crisis, investors immediately fled the asset class as the effects of the so-called Tequila Crisis spread across the board.

The crisis triggered a panic attack in Washington. It had only been a few years, in some cases a few months, since these countries exited the debt crisis, and now they were about to return to the abyss. The United States had just ratified a Free Trade Agreement with Mexico (NAFTA), and it was in the process of embarking on similar treaties with a host of other developing countries. Washington was realizing that as the only hegemon, it could not allow the global system to slip out of its hands. For the first three months of 1995, the Clinton administration worked valiantly to convince the United States Congress to establish a bailout fund for Mexico, but it was to no avail. Finally, the Federal Reserve, along with the multilateral lending agencies, organized a rescue plan that partially used obscure currency swap lines to save Mexico. Calling themselves the International Fire Brigade, US Treasury Secretary Robert Rubin and Deputy Secretary Larry Summers used the Mexican precedent to provide temporary support for other emerging market countries in distress.

The idea was to provide rescue packages that exceeded market expectations. Hence, investors would return to the field. Washington was now playing a new game. It was more interested in signaling confidence to the markets as the way to shape investor behavior. Argentina could have exited the Convertibility Plan during the 1995 crisis, which would have avoided much of the turmoil that came later. However, President Menem was too busy changing the constitution so that he could have another chance at the presidency. Therefore, there was no way he was going to plunge the country into an economic crisis on the eve of his campaign. Under an agreement known as the Pact of Olivos, the Radicals agreed to allow reelection in return for reducing the presidential term from six years to four. It also permitted each of the provinces to be represented by a third senator from the first minority party, and it granted complete legislative autonomy to the city of Buenos Aires—a bastion of Radical political support.

Menem's reelection coincided with a short revival of the emerging markets as investors returned to pick up assets on the cheap. With the knowledge that Washington would backstop developing countries if they got into trouble, the investment community decided to throw caution to the wind. It was a good example of a moral hazard problem, whereby investors ignore fundamental analysis in the knowledge that they will be bailed out by the official sector. In the meantime, the Argentine economy was back on the mend. The last of the privatizations were finalized, and GDP growth accelerated to a pace of 8.4 percent year on year in 1997. Unfortunately, the reverberations of the Tequila Crisis were making their way to the other side of the globe and shaking the foundations of Southeast Asia. The so-called Asian Tigers also pegged their currencies to the dollar, which allowed them to stabilize, attract capital inflows, and accelerate GDP growth. However, the risk aversion that resulted from the Mexican crisis hit the Asian Tigers hard. Struggling with overvalued currencies and enormous current account deficits, they were forced to devalue their exchange rates, thus triggering a tsunami of corporate restructurings. The Asian Crisis sparked new concerns about countries with similar difficulties, and the downturn boomeranged back to the other side of the globe.

It was clear that Argentina had problems with its external accounts. The appreciating peso made the country lose its economic competitiveness, resulting in diminished foreign direct investment.[82] Therefore, it had to rely more on the international bond market to meet its external obligations. To that end, it needed to have a strong sponsor. Fortunately, the IMF and World Bank filled the role. In 1998, President Menem was invited to address the annual meeting in Washington to present the country's successful economic program. Investors interpreted the event as a huge endorsement of the multilaterals' commitment to Argentina, and they continued to plow money into the country despite Russia's devaluation of the ruble in 1998 and the end of Brazil's Real Plan in 1999. Nevertheless, a small cadre of economists argued that Argentina would eventually have to throw in the towel. In 1999, Fernando de la Rua, a Radical from Cordoba, was elected president. In an effort to keep the currency board afloat and regain competitiveness, he turned to the former architects

---

82 Rodolfo Terragno, *Privatizaciones en la Argentina* (Buenos Aires: Fundacion Omega Seguros, 2000), 56.

of the Austral Plan, José Luis Machinea and Ricardo Lopez Murphy, to embark the country on a painful deflationary program by cutting benefits, wages, and tariffs.

The measures pushed the Argentine economy into a death spiral; it contracted 3.1 percent year on year in 1999, 0.5 percent year on year in 2000, and 4.5 percent year on year in 2001. The move into negative territory shut down Argentina's access to institutional investors. Therefore, the government began to rely more on private banking issues and selling bonds to wealthy Argentines, Italians, and Germans. At the same time, the multilaterals continued drumming up their support for the Argentine government by encouraging investors to participate in deals. They also made up for the shortfall by generous lending facilities. In other words, the multilaterals were slowly becoming the largest creditor group to the country. Realizing that their own capital was at stake, Washington began talking about the need for bail-ins rather than bailouts. Led by a young Harvard economist, Nouriel Roubini, the US Treasury argued that any further bailout of Argentina would require private sector participation.

The shift in Washington's attitude toward Argentina coincided with a change in the White House. After stewing for eight years on the sidelines, the Republicans were voted back into office. As is often the case, an incoming opposition party often takes a polar opposite stance on many issues. There is a saying in politics: the friend of my enemy is my enemy. Several senior Republicans had a great deal of resentment against the Clinton administration's notion of an international fire brigade. They railed against the risks of moral hazard and the damage it had on market discipline. Topping the list was

Argentina. The Republicans argued that it was in an unsustainable position that would end in disaster.

Previously, the Argentine government was given an enormous amount of latitude in meeting its IMF goals, but now there was no slack. President de la Rua knew that the situation was desperate. Therefore, in March 2001, he reappointed the architect of the Convertibility Plan, Domingo Cavallo, to the Ministry of the Economy. Cavallo immediately went into action securing emergency powers from Congress to enact special measures. In addition to the lack of competitiveness and the dearth of financing opportunities, the government again faced a persistent deficit in the fiscal accounts. This time the hole was the result of two new structural flaws. The first was the privatization of the pension fund system. Although Argentines were saving toward their own retirement, creating an important pool of domestic capital, the government still had to provide benefits for the people who were retired. This created a double strain on the fiscal accounts, since the government could no longer count on the contributions from people who were in the workforce. The second flaw was the coparticipation laws that had been established at San Nicolas.

When Buenos Aires and the provinces ended their struggle and agreed to share government revenues, the provinces took a large portion of the public purse. Efforts to raise taxes were diluted because large proportions of the funds were immediately shared. In an effort to plug the hole, Cavallo increased the export tariffs on grains and introduced a check debit tax. However, neither of the revenues was coparticipated. By using his special powers, he passed legislation that would keep the additional revenues at the federal level.

The new measures were good, and there was some hope that the IMF would continue supporting the Argentine government. However, the die was cast. In August 2001, Treasury Secretary Paul O'Neill went so far as to say during a television interview that he did not want the tax dollars of US plumbers and carpenters wasted on a country whose citizens did not even pay their own taxes. It was clear that the end was nigh. The same investment banks that previously completed bond deals and privatizations for the Argentine government began to parade small groups of fund managers through the offices of the Treasury to hear that the United States would no longer support additional bailouts. This convinced US fund managers to sell down their positions prior to the onset of the debacle. Hence, an Argentine default would not repeat the damage that the debt crisis of the 1980s had done to the US financial system.

To make matters worse, Washington's attitude toward Argentina hardened in September 2001 after terrorists used hijacked airplanes to demolish the World Trade Center in New York. The Bush administration swiveled its attention toward the Middle East, and Latin America was abandoned.

The final days of the year were a whirlwind of headlines as the Argentine government concocted ways to service its external obligations. The straightjacket of the Convertibility Plan was now a noose around its neck. As investors fled for the door and Argentines took their money out of the banks, the level of international reserves fell, thus shrinking the money supply. As a result, the economy went into a deflationary spiral, with no way of being able to break out of the spin.

Unable to secure external help, the government tried to squeeze as much as it could from domestic resources. It launched a Patriotic Bond in order to force banks and firms to help service its needs. It tried to force Governor Nestor Kirchner of the province of Santa Cruz to repatriate the oil revenues he held in offshore Swiss bank accounts. Unfortunately, it was to no avail. In December 2001, the IMF refused to provide additional waivers, and there was an immediate run on the banks. With the economy in free fall, Cavallo tendered his resignation, and President de la Rua resigned and escaped in the presidential helicopter. Mayhem ensued. People sacked supermarkets, attacked the banks, and set government buildings ablaze. The Ministry of the Economy and the Congress were torched. Many families fled the country. During two weeks in January, the country went through a succession of five presidents before falling into the hands of Buenos Aires Governor Eduardo Duhalde.

Many people considered Duhalde to be the real mastermind behind de la Rua's collapse. Even though the country was suffering the worst economic crisis of its history, de la Rua could have remained in control if he could have counted on the backing of the governors and of Congress. However, Duhalde sensed the president's weakness and organized a virtual coup by removing all support. It was a replay of the previous Radical administrations, all of which had fallen into the hands of the military or the Peronists. Finally, when Duhalde gained control of the presidency, he was allowed to serve out the remainder of de la Rua's term.

Argentina's tryst with liberalism was a disaster. The government was in shambles and the economy wrecked. The country defaulted on almost $100 billion in foreign debt, and the currency dropped by more than 75 percent. With many of the privatization contracts dollarized, the government was forced to abrogate them. Faced with the loss of essential services, it was forced to nationalize some of the privatized companies. Household savings were also wiped out. The financial system was destroyed, and most corporations were forced to file for bankruptcy protection. Ironically, this should have been the turning point for Argentina. Had it been allowed to survive for six more months, it would have emerged from the crisis.

Two important events took place on the eve of the collapse. The first event was China's accession to the World Trade Organization (WTO) in November 2001. From that moment on, commodity prices soared as the behemoth rejoined the global economic community after a half-century hiatus. The second event was the terrorist attacks of September 11, 2001. Given the shock to the global financial system caused by those attacks, the Federal Reserve cut interest rates to zero. This allowed the dollar to depreciate sharply. Because the Argentine peso was linked to the dollar, its value would have fallen, too. For the next decade, the greenback was one of the weakest currencies on the planet—which would have been a boon for the Argentine economy.

In sum, Argentina was lured by the promises of liberalism. It sold off its state-owned assets. It indebted itself with international investors and allowed itself to be used as a pawn to attract other developing countries to do the same. In the end, it was unceremoniously dumped. Argentina was no longer a stellar example of proper economic management; instead, it was the paradigm of mismanagement. Many considered it a failed state even though it had followed the rules suggested from abroad.

Water and Oil

Shunned by the international community and with its economy in tatters, Argentina was forced to pull itself up from the floor. The Convertibility Plan, which had been the institutional mainstay for the past decade, was gone. With no access to international capital, the only way it could survive was by returning to its areas of comparative advantage. The reintegration of the Chinese economy into the global marketplace brought new life to the commodity markets. With an abundance of potable water, Argentina was well positioned to take advantage of the increase in grain prices. The discovery of oil and shale-gas deposits in Neuquén provided the country with the potential to become a major energy producer. The combination of water and oil would have major implications for the future development of the Argentine economy as the country neared its bicentennial celebrations.

The Argentine default sent shock waves throughout the developing world. Argentina was the IMF's star pupil, but

it was now a pariah. Losing faith in the asset class, investors fled from other emerging countries such as Chile and
Peru. There was a severe backlash in Washington against the
intransigent position and highly politicized decisions pursued
by the US Treasury. As a result, foreign economic policymaking reverted to the State Department, which pursued a more
balanced approach. Yet, the damage was done. The valu-
ation of the Brazilian real and Colombian peso plunged as
investors bolted. To many in the Bush administration, Argentina was an isolated outpost with little strategic significance.
Therefore, it was expendable. Its economic collapse did not
have an immediate impact on US regional interests.

Brazil and Colombia were viewed as having greater importance than Argentina. Brazil was the largest country in South
America and a traditional ally of the United States. US corporations had enormous operations in Brazil, and that country
was the source of strategic raw materials such as iron ore
and timber. Likewise, Colombia was dealing with a three-
decade-long struggle against a narco-funded insurgency. An
economic crisis in Colombia would convert the third largest
country in South America into a regional threat that would
imperil US commercial, political, and military interests. For
these reasons, the United States decided to lead an assistance program for the region despite its abhorrence of previous efforts. The main recipients of the funds were Colombia
and Brazil, both of which received a combined $50 billion in
multilateral assistance.

In the meantime, the Argentine government tried to pick
up the pieces. Under the leadership of President Duhalde,
the government put in place emergency measures to steady
the financial system. Dollar-value CDs and loans were forci-

bly converted into pesos. Sight deposits were prolonged into longer-term instruments in a process that became known as the *corralito*. Bankruptcy proceedings were suspended, and exchange rate controls were imposed. Under the guiding hand of Economy Minister Roberto Lavagna, the Argentine economy began to stabilize. Yet, elections were looming on the horizon in 2003, and Duhalde needed a successor. His idea was to pick a weak candidate so he could manipulate him from the sidelines. Several leading political figures were approached, but all of them declined because they knew what he had in mind. At the same time, former President Menem was making another dash for the presidency. Running out of time, Duhalde turned to Nestor Kirchner. Besides being the governor of Santa Cruz and holding $500 million of the province's oil royalties in an offshore Swiss bank account, Kirchner had a relatively low profile. A lawyer by training and a lifelong Peronist, he had been a member of the Peronist youth movement during the military regime. Most people considered him politically weak, and they thought he would be a caretaker until Duhalde could run again in 2007.

Given the political vacuum that existed in the aftermath of the crisis, several candidates decided to throw their hats into the ring. As a result, the electoral slate was full, and the results were fragmented. Menem led the pack with 24 percent of the vote, followed by Kirchner with 22 percent. Under Argentine electoral rules, the candidates would square off a second time in a process commonly known as the *ballotage*. However, the public opinion polls showed a very high rejection rate for Menem. Given his association with the Convertibility Plan and his liberal economic policies, he had no chance of winning the *ballotage*. Therefore, he abruptly abandoned his campaign, thus allowing Kirchner to declare victory with only 22 percent of the vote. Upon taking office, Kirchner surprised everyone by being more astute than he appeared. One of the first things he did was to reappoint Lavagna as minister of the economy, and then the two of them restructured the defaulted sovereign bonds.

The US government and the multilaterals were pressuring Argentina to accelerate the restructuring process. They urged Buenos Aires to apply a deep discount to the new instruments, which would force investors to bear the brunt of the pain. The decision to do so was not out of malicious intent toward the investment community. It was done so that the multilateral lending agencies would not be forced to assume any losses. Argentina's debt load following the devaluation was a prodigious 185 percent of GDP. Of the $165 billion in foreign obligations, approximately $100 billion was in bonds, and most of the remainder was in multilateral and bilateral loans. In order to minimize their losses, it was necessary to impose a larger write-off on the private sector's positions. Washington knew that this would not trigger a political backlash, given that most of the largest US institutional investors were no longer involved. They had been duly warned about the looming default. Hence, the losses would not have an impact on the US financial system. Most of the debt was now held by Argentine citizens and private European investors.

The Argentine government offered a deal to bondholders that would allow them to receive new instruments worth twenty-four cents on the dollar. Like the Brady Plan, the new restructuring plan carried a menu of options that allowed investors to receive par bonds and discount bonds, as well as local currency debentures. As an added incentive, bondholders were given one GDP warrant for each dollar they tendered. The GDP warrant was an innovative instrument that was similar to an equity kicker. The government recognized that during the past thirty years, the Argentine economy had grown an average of 3 percent year on year. However, given that the large reduction in debt would allow it to grow at a faster pace, the GDP warrant allowed investors to share in the upside. The instrument had a maximum payout of forty-eight cents. Therefore, the true haircut of the Argentine restructuring was less than the seventy-six cents that was widely advertised. Investors recovered the twenty-four cents of the bonds plus the net present value of the forty-eight cents in warrant payments. Unfortunately, not everyone received the payouts. After six months, the instruments were detachable, and many investors sold them for pennies on the dollar.

Few people realized that the Argentine economy would take off as soon as the dust from the crisis settled. Unencumbered by the prodigious debt load, armed with a hyper-competitive exchange rate, and enjoying an unprecedented commodity boom, the Argentine economy flew. In 2003, Argentina grew 8.6 percent year on year. In 2004, it expanded 9 percent year on year, and the growth rate would stay above 8.5 percent year on year for the next three years. Even though the country was an outcast, it enjoyed the same performance as it did at its economic zenith.

Just as it had done a century earlier, Argentina became a global leader in agriculture, particularly in grain technology. Argentine agronomists and farmers became renowned for their advances in seed genetics and farming techniques. At the end of the 1990s, the agricultural sector embraced genetically modified (GM) seeds as a way to reduce costs by minimizing pesticide use. Argentine laboratories began developing and producing domestic variants for local and international markets. Another innovative advance was the move to no-till farming. By employing special equipment to cut a thin groove in the topsoil, which was injected with seed and fertilizer, farmers slashed operational costs, reduced erosion, and conserved water. The job opportunities generated by the agricultural sector prodded Argentine universities into preparing students for a wide range of agrarian specialties. There were also advances in agro-related industrial output. Factories churned out top-of-the-line tractors, and Argentine companies, such as Molinos Rio de la Plata and Vicentin, became dominant players in the global food- and grain-processing industries.

Using the infrastructure that had been modernized during Menem's term, Argentina enjoyed a superior advantage to its giant neighbor to the north. Its ports were among the most efficient in the world, having been sold a decade earlier to Asian owners. Its river system allowed an efficient form of fluvial transportation to move grains from the verdant regions of Cordoba and Santa Fe to the bustling ports of Buenos Aires and Rosario. The remnants of the British-built railroad system also allowed farmers to move their products to market. Still behind the efficiency of their US counterparts, the Argentines were able to take advantage of their lower labor costs and favorable growing conditions to become the second largest exporter of processed soybeans and to secure an important slice of the global grain market.

Fleets of heavily laden ships navigated the muddy waters of the River Plate after each harvest season, headed for the burgeoning markets of Asia, the Middle East, and the former

Soviet Union. Major international commodity firms, such as Bunge & Born, Cargill, and Louis Dreyfus operated huge facilities generating billions of dollars in revenues. With such a steady inflow of hard currency, the Argentine government was no longer dependent on the international capital markets. Indeed, its problem was too many dollars flowing into the central bank's vault and appreciating the value of the peso. Therefore, in 2004, the government began a program of exchange rate intervention, which led to a steady accumulation of international reserves.

Likewise, the Argentine government no longer felt that it needed to defer to the international financial community or the multilateral lending agencies. Hence, the Kirchner Administration developed an antagonistic bias toward them and blamed the IMF, the World Bank, and Wall Street for its woes. This heightened the country's financial isolation. It was bad enough that it had suffered the largest sovereign default, but now the government was taking deliberate steps to rile the investor community.

The antipathy of the government toward liberalism was not based on ideology, but on political necessity. Sensing the political void that resulted from the crisis, the mild-mannered Kirchner blossomed into a political animal. He pulled out the stops to centralize as much power as possible and keep it within his grip by using the Peronist apparatus to convert the greater Buenos Aires region into his political citadel and his family into the country's main dynasty. Moreover, the booming economy boosted his standing, and he enjoyed enormous popularity and support. He was also very shrewd in his use of the Peronist machine. Through political patronage and clientelism, he used the unions to threaten wayward industrialists. He deployed gangs of thugs known as the *piqueteros* to intimidate the population. They held impromptu protest marches in the middle of the city and brought traffic to a standstill. His technique was one of physical coercion: He used government ministers to threaten politicians, business leaders, and individuals who refused to comply with his policies and edicts.

At the same time, he created an inner circle of industrial allies, most of whom received previously privatized companies from multinationals that were desperate to flee the chaotic economic environment. These operations were divested at knockdown prices and capitalized with the latest technology and machinery. In order to clean up their balance sheets, the government passed legislation that allowed the new owners to restructure their debts without diluting their equity stakes—thus generating untold wealth for a handful of political allies. Because of these measures, Kirchner was able to consolidate his power base to become lord and master of Argentina.

Unwilling to waste his political capital, Kirchner launched his wife, Cristina Fernandez de Kirchner, as his successor in the 2007 presidential elections. Like her husband, Fernandez was a lawyer and a staunch Peronist. She was reelected to Congress many times when they lived in Santa Cruz, and she was known to be a fiery orator. Kirchner knew very well that he could sit on the sidelines and return to the presidency later. By doing so, he and his wife could rule the country for at least sixteen years, and perhaps even more if they groomed their son to continue the dynasty.

Fernandez ran on a platform of continuity against a mixed field of Radicals and traditional Peronists. With the wind at her back, the economy soaring, and grain prices in the stratosphere, she easily won the race. Most political analysts thought that the new president would assume a more moderate position in regards to economic policymaking. The emerging markets rally was in full swing, and capital was flowing into neighboring countries. A more conciliatory tone would allow Argentina to share in the bonanza of foreign investment. It would allow the economy to enjoy a consumer boom that would surely bolster Fernandez's popular support and assure her reelection in 2011. However, she decided to go the other way. Instead of softening her stance against liberalism, she redoubled it—taking an even more aggressive interventionist line. In 2008, she tried to strengthen her economic base by taking on the agricultural sector and increasing the export tariffs on grains. For the first time in decades, an Argentine president decided to go head to head against the powerful agricultural lobby.

Ever since the troubled days of 2001, when Economy Minister Cavallo obtained special executive powers to deal with the crisis, the government was able to collect all of the revenue generated by the export tariffs without having to share it with the provinces. It was a return to the early days of the viceroyalty when Buenos Aires enjoyed the fruits produced by the entire colony without having to split them with anyone else. Cavallo introduced the tariff measures as a means to generate more revenues to service external obligations, but now those revenues served as a windfall for the federal government. The bonanza allowed Kirchner to solidify his political base by increasing the benefits and social services provided to the working poor who resided on the outskirts of the capital. They were given food vouchers, subsidized electricity, and transportation along with additional handouts. The largess of the federal government was done at the cost of the provinces and the agricultural sector. Farmers begrudgingly went along with Cavallo's initial emergency measures, but Fernandez's attempt to increase the tariffs was just too much. Her government proposed a movable scale that permitted the retention rates to increase as grain prices went up, thus allowing it to enjoy more of the upside.

Although some vestiges of the landed aristocracy were still present, the Argentine agricultural sector changed dramatically during the last decade of the twentieth century. Many traditional families sold their farms during the Convertibility Plan, taking the opportunity to lock in better prices for their properties and move their money offshore. Corporations, cooperatives, and professional farmers gradually took over. This reduced the nexus between the military and the landed aristocracy, a process that followed the defeat in the Malvinas. After the war, Menem professionalized the armed forces, eliminated conscription, and opened access to the officer corps. Therefore, there was no fear that the agricultural sector would join arms with the military to oust the president, as had occurred during previous confrontations. Nevertheless, the agricultural sector did not stand idly by. The alteration of the tariff scheme was the undermining of the coparticipation mechanism that had been hammered out at the bloody battles of Caseros, San Nicolas, and Pavon. In contrast, the tariff scheme was the institutional mechanism by which the provinces coalesced into a unified state. Therefore, the reaction was going to be hard.

Farmers quickly mobilized. There were disruptions to food supplies, and fleets of tractors clogged the streets of Buenos Aires. In the end, the legislative initiative was defeated. In a dramatic scene, the Peronist members of the legislature locked arms and tied the opposition. However, the tie-breaking vote was cast by none other than the vice president, Julio Cobos—a member of the Radical Party. Cobos was appointed to the vice presidency as a sign of bipartisanship and national reconciliation. President Fernandez would ultimately rue the day that she made this move, and it would color her attitude toward any future attempt at accommodation.

For the rest of her time in office, she would pursue a more confrontational style of management. Instead of looking for consensus and discussing issues in open debates, she relied on a close circle of friends, ignored her cabinet, and dismantled the remaining independent institutions. Rather than using capable technocrats to manage the country's ministries, she turned to loyal puppets in the Ministry of the Economy and the Central Bank. In addition to political aggression, Fernandez undertook a policy of manipulation. This manifested itself in various ways. One of them was the alteration of the country's economic indices to paint a more favorable picture to the public. The most alarming incident centered on the Consumer Price Index (CPI) that was produced by the national statistics agency, INDEC.

The government's constant intervention in the currency market to keep the peso from appreciating led to an expansion of the money supply and upward pressure on consumer prices. At the same time, the government provided generous salary increases to compensate for the postdevaluation loss in real wages. It was a way to maintain the support of the unions and working poor. Unfortunately, the expansion in the money supply and the constant rise in wages led to large increases in the inflation rate. Unwilling to take the painful fiscal and monetary measures needed to stem the inflationary spike, the government began to fudge the indices. The situation came to a head in March 2007 when the director responsible for the calculation of the consumer price index, Graciela Bevacqua, was fired after she tried to publish a number that was higher than the government wanted. The incident sent powerful shockwaves through the market. At issue was not only the fact that the government was cooking the books; a large component of the newly restructured bonds paid interest rates that were based on inflation. Investors immediately dumped positions when they realized that they were being shortchanged. In response to the doubts about the official numbers, several private economists began publishing their own inflation estimates. The government reacted harshly by fining any published inflation estimate that differed from government sources. Even the IMF became involved in the matter, threatening to censure the country if it responded to concerns about the quality of its economic statistics.

In 2008, Fernandez took her aggressive style of governing to a higher level by nationalizing the private pension fund system, AFJP. With $30 billion in pension assets on her doorstep, the private pension funds were too tempting to leave alone. At the end of 2008, the government swept up all of the assets into the only remaining state-owned pension fund, ANSES, thus providing the government with a treasure trove of resources to meet its internal and external obligations. In actuality, the nationalization of the AFJPs may have been justified. The private pension fund managers charged very high commissions, and there was very little variance in the performance of the portfolios. Nevertheless, the way that it was nationalized affirmed the authoritarian style of the president. There was no open consultation or debate on the issue, and many senior officials in the Ministry of the Economy were ignorant of the government's intent until they read it in the morning newspaper.

In addition to the heavy-handed treatment of economic statistics and the pension fund system, another hallmark of her government was the manipulation of the media. Initially, President Kirchner and his wife enjoyed a cozy relationship with the press, even allowing Clarin, the biggest media group in the country, to proceed with a controversial merger that brought together two of the biggest cable companies, Cablevision and Multicanal. The merger created the largest media group in Argentina. However, the management of Clarin grew tired of the Kirchners' despotic tactics and became vocal critics of the government's policies. They became strident supporters of the farmers' fight against the increase in agricultural tariffs, but this led to a violent backlash from President Fernandez. In December 2009, Congress passed the Law on Audio-Visual Communications, also known as the media law, which revamped the whole sector. The ownership of the broadcast market was split into three segments: private companies, state-owned entities, and nonprofit organizations. As a result, the government annulled the merger between Cablevision and Multicanal, and Clarin was ordered to divest itself of many of its cable assets. Yet, despite her aggressive style, Fernandez remained popular. Argentines have always had a penchant for strong leaders. Furthermore, the impressive performance of the Argentine economy allowed her to shower the masses with generous subsidies and transfers, but the abundance generated by the commodity boom was driven by factors that were totally outside of her control.

The rally in commodity prices was obviously welcomed by regional leaders, but it took a while for them to associate it with the ascendency of China. With the exception of Chile, Latin American trade with Asia was minimal at the start of the twenty-first century. In 2001, when China was admitted into the WTO, several financial commentators and Wall Street analysts began discussing the positive impact that the acceleration of the Chinese economy would have on commodity prices and raw materials producers. While the region was still embroiled in the fallout from the Argentine crisis in 2001, Goldman Sachs analyst Jim O'Neill wrote a paper that forecasted a new era of prosperity for the developing world.[83] He argued that the principal beneficiaries would consist of Brazil, Russia, India, and China (BRIC). His acronym was mainly a marketing ploy to highlight the opportunities provided by emerging market financial instruments. In reality, the only country that was driving the transformation was China. India was still generations behind as it struggled to develop a political consensus to liberalize the economy and embrace the necessary reforms to open its economy. Russia was trying to recover from a century of communism, and Brazil was absconded behind a wall of protectionism, deep-seated corruption, and a byzantine bureaucratic network. Other economies would benefit more from the ascendency of China, such as Chile, Indonesia, and Peru. However, they lacked the scale and range of financial instruments that would make them interesting to investors.

---

83 James O'Neill, *Building Better Global Economic BRICs* (Goldman Sachs, 2001).

Initially, Latin American policymakers were reluctant to spend the commodity-produced windfall. They had recently emerged from the Lost Decade of the 1980s, the roller coaster ride of the 1990s, and the debacle of the Argentine default. Since the end of the Second World War, there had been episodes of rising commodity prices, but the rallies proved to be fleeting. Therefore, the governments did not do much more than use the windfall to pay down debt, improve reserve levels, and bolster their fiscal accounts. Indeed, policymakers did not realize until 2004 and 2005 that they were witnessing a structural change in the global economy.

It is important to note that the spike in China's demand for agricultural products was not only due to its growing prosperity; it was also the result of the changes altering the country's industrial landscape. When China sought to reintegrate into the global economy, its industrial base was destroyed and bereft of capital. All it had at its disposal was a huge mass of cheap labor. Therefore, Beijing began offering incentives for multinational manufacturers to establish operations in China. These incentives took the form of free land and favorable labor contracts. This started in the 1980s and accelerated during the 1990s, and in the process, China developed a network of suppliers and producers that allowed it to dominate narrow industrial sectors.

However, China is also a major producer of commodities. Manchuria is chocked with minerals, the Yellow River Valley is an important agricultural region, and the country is the world's largest source of rare earth minerals. During the initial part of the postwar period, China was mostly autarkic. Yet, commodity consumption was low because of the depressed levels of economic activity. As manufacturing output increased,

China could no longer rely on its domestic resources, and it was forced to import raw materials to expand its industry and modernize its infrastructure. In addition to energy and metals, the demand for agricultural products increased as the Chinese population became more prosperous. China's per capita income during the early 1980s was below the average for sub-Saharan Africa, but the increase in output augmented real wages. This allowed households to improve their dietary intakes. To illustrate the point, Chinese consumption of soybeans jumped 160 percent between 2000 and 2011 as local farmers increased their use of the grain to expand meat production. Lacking the domestic supply to satisfy the increased demand, the country turned to the import market.

Water was one of the commodities in particularly short supply. Most of the western regions of China are arid. As a result, the population is corralled along the coastline where the land is arable and there is a better supply of potable water. However, there is not enough to adequately sustain the population, irrigate the crops, and support a mammoth manufacturing base. To put things in context, the Chinese government estimates that total renewable water resources are 2.8 trillion cubic meters.[84] This translates to 2,150 cubic meters of water per inhabitant; this compares poorly with the United States, which has seven thousand cubic meters per inhabitant, and Argentina with twenty-one thousand cubic meters. The situation becomes even more acute when agricultural needs are considered.

Agro production is very intensive in its use of water. For example, one bushel of corn requires fifteen cubic meters

---

84 Velma Grover, *Water: A Source of Conflict or Cooperation* (Enfield: Science Publishers, 2007), 69-71.

of water, a bushel of wheat needs forty-two cubic meters of water, and a bushel of soybeans requires fifty-one cubic meters. This is in contrast to the use of water in industrial processes. For example, the manufacturing of an automobile requires 147 cubic meters of water. Given the enormous size of the population, the growth in prosperity, and the increased industrial output, China was draining its water resources. A good illustration was observed in the North China Plain. The demands on the Yellow River were so high that it dried up before reaching the Bohai Sea, thus forcing farmers to rely much more on nonrenewable aquifers to meet their needs.[85]

The use of agricultural imports was not only a means to augment the limited supply of domestic products. It was a way to redirect more of its water resources into human and manufacturing use.[86] Annual soybean imports jumped to forty-one million metric tons in 2010 from 136 thousand metric tons in 1992. Annual corn imports reached four million metric tons in 2010, which was more than the accumulated amount it had imported during the previous twenty-five years. The import of grains and other food products became a proxy for importing the liquid. Instead of filling supertankers with water to irrigate farms, the Chinese imported the final product. In the process, it was able to employ its domestic aquatic sources for other industrial processes.

As grain prices soared, Argentine farmers cultivated land that was farther away from the traditional transportation hubs. The biggest move was to the northeast as farmers

85 Peter Orszag, "Why We Care About the Price of Water in China," *Bloomberg Magazine* (July 6, 2011).
86 Elizabeth Economy, "China's Growing Water Crisis," *World Politics Review* (August 9, 2011).

took advantage of the huge Guarani Aquifer that sat under the provinces of Cordoba, Entre Rios, and Missiones. As a result, thirty million hectares of land were converted to farm use. Much of the expansion was done by local farmers, but some of it was led by Chinese and foreign investors, which triggered a political backlash. Some Argentines worried that Chinese companies would snap up too much farmland in a sort of quasi invasion. Hence, the government introduced legislation limiting how much land foreigners could own. Nevertheless, there was a perception that the agro boom would last forever. Unfortunately, the rally would derail at the end of 2008 with the collapse of Lehman Brothers.

The seeds of the Lehman debacle were sown well before the start of the US financial crisis. For years, the Federal Reserve pursued a lax monetary approach. In the process, it created a series of asset bubbles. The trend began in the early 1990s when Federal Reserve Chairman Alan Greenspan allowed the US unemployment rate to fall below 5 percent without raising interest rates. Traditionally, it regarded a level of 5 percent as the minimum unemployment rate that would not fuel inflationary pressures. Formally known as the Non-Accelerating Inflation Rate of Unemployment (NAIRU), it was the boundary where the market anticipated that the Federal Reserve would begin to tighten monetary policy. Greenspan argued that technological changes and improvements in labor productivity allowed the NAIRU to be lower. In one regard, he was right. Inflation did not rise as the unemployment rate dropped below 5 percent. However, on a different note, it reduced risk aversion as investors looked for new ways to bolster returns. This led to a series of asset bubbles. The first one occurred in the emerging markets during the latter part of the 1990s. It was followed by the Internet craze at the turn of the century and the subprime mortgage lending bubble during the 2000s. The excess liquidity was exacerbated by the Fed's approach to exogenous shocks, such as the collapse of the dot-com bubble, the millennium bug, and the terrorist attacks of September 11, 2001. After each incident, the Fed opened up the monetary taps and flooded the markets with money, which led to even more speculation.

Of the three shocks, the response to the terrorist attacks produced the biggest impact. The Federal Reserve cut interest rates to zero. As the cloud of debris settled in lower Manhattan, US households took advantage of the low rates to refinance mortgages, modernize dwellings, and purchase new homes. The easy credit conditions soon turned into a whirlwind of unrestrained property speculation, and by the mid-2000s, real estate prices were soaring. Banks aggressively peddled loans to unqualified buyers who were commonly categorized as subprime borrowers. They represented the most lucrative part of the market since they paid the highest interest rates and generated the largest fees. By the end of 2006, the banks were in an orgy of issuing risky mortgages, repackaging them, and selling them to a variety of domestic and international investors. Given that the loans were bundled together in order to minimize risk, the credit rating agencies used statistical models to rate them as safe. Consequently, they were sought out by institutional investors who needed highly rated instruments to meet regulatory requirements. For years, the abundance of easy credit allowed the US property market to fly, but things started coming apart in 2007. Delinquencies were on the rise, and property prices were out of reach for many households. By 2008, cracks began to appear in the US financial monolith. In March 2008, Bear Stearns collapsed, and it was forced into the hands of JP Morgan. By September, Lehman Brothers was brought to its knees. The once-great firm sought bankruptcy protection.

The collapse of Lehman sent powerful reverberations throughout the global financial system, bringing transactions to a halt and pushing the economy into recession. Commodity prices plunged at the end of 2008 and early 2009, halting the Argentine expansion. GDP growth was a meager 1.3 percent year on year in 2009. Fortunately, a series of stimulus programs across the developing world, particularly in China, as well as a set of heterodox policies in the United States, allowed the global economy to recover by the end of the year.

With the US economy limping along and Europe facing mounting concerns about its southern flank, many investors sought safety in the emerging world. Developing countries were no longer perceived as outposts for specialists, and many consultants began advising institutional investors to allocate funds to emerging market assets. As a result, more money began flowing into Latin America, Eastern Europe, Africa, and Asia. Realizing that it was losing an excellent opportunity to attract more capital, Argentina took steps to normalize its relationship with the international financial community. The government promised to settle with the Paris Club, and it reopened the exchange to bring in the remaining bondholders who did not participate in the original deal. The terms were very similar to the original package, except the government recognized the Past Due Interest (PDI) that had accrued since the previous offer. Because of the generous terms, the government tendered an additional 20 percent of the defaulted bonds. This mainly consisted of the retail European investors who did not participate in the initial exchange, as well as some distressed hedge funds. The remaining outstanding bondholders were mainly vulture funds seeking to recover the entire value of the bonds. The Ministry of the Economy knew they would hinder its future access to the international capital markets. Hence, it ultimately needed to be resolved. Fortunately, grain prices were on the rise, and the government was not in need of any external financing.

As Argentina approached its bicentennial, oil engineers and geologists were studying the scrubland just south of the pampas in a region known as Vaca Muerta. Hydrocarbon sediments were known to exist along the foothills of the Andes, but the deposits were small and imbedded in porous rock formations. Fortunately, new advances in drilling and production technologies were allowing the extraction of these hydrocarbons to become economically feasible. The most important change was the advent of hydraulic fracturing technology—also known as fracking. The technique was pioneered by George P. Mitchell in Texas. Geologists and oil engineers were always intrigued by the large deposits of oil and gas that were embedded in shale, but extraction was difficult. During the 1970s, engineers and wildcatters began using new equipment and methods to perform directional drilling. Instead of boring a hole straight into the ground, the new equipment allowed them to make turns and drill horizontally, thus opening up fresh possibilities to exploit the hydrocarbon deposits that were scattered along a rock formation. Armed with new technology, Mitchell drilled horizontally and pumped high-pressure sandy water into the soft rock to break it apart. This allowed the particles to wedge open the fissures. Using perforated pipes, Mitchell was then able to capture the embedded gas and oil. As a result, the new technique revolutionized the US energy industry.

There were some important drawbacks to fracking. To begin, it was environmentally dangerous. Not only did it leave a large residue of polluted water; it contaminated the ground water and aquifers. It was for this reason that many of the large European countries rejected it. Given the large empty tracts of land in the western parts of the United States, the country was able to exploit its shale resources without affecting the population. Argentina also found itself in similar conditions. The stretches below the Rio Negro are relatively desolate, and they are not part of the pampas. Therefore, they can suffer the environmental damage produced by fracking without causing human hardships. It would take some time for engineers to grasp the extent of the hydrocarbon deposits in Vaca Muerta, but it would have important implications for the future of YPF and the role of Argentina on the global energy stage.

Despite the ignominious collapse of the Convertibility Plan, the Argentine economy showed an enormous resilience in recovering from the economic crisis. It did so by returning to its areas of comparative advantage. Fortunately, it was well positioned to benefit from the reincorporation of China into the global community by becoming a major exporter of agricultural products. It was another way of maximizing its abundant hydro resources by exporting water-based products. The advent of fracking technology also allowed Argentina to move into the vanguard of oil and gas, and it could become one of the energy powerhouses of the twenty-first century.

A Bicentennial of Development

On May 25, 2010, Argentina celebrated its bicentennial with leagues of foreign dignitaries, fireworks displays, and rock concerts. The event marked a major milestone for a nation that started as a distant outpost of a vast empire. When studying Argentina's turbulent history, it is undeniable that geography has been the single most important factor that has shaped its governmental structure, its leadership, and its future. Understanding the challenges and opportunities of this vast land goes a long way to deciphering many of the policy decisions that have been made.

The convergence of the three major rivers that drain much of South America created one of the largest estuaries on the planet. The founding of Buenos Aires at the end of the estuary endowed the city with a privileged geographic position. From its shores, it could intercept all vessels that sailed upriver toward the provinces that supported the rich mining operations of Potosi, thus becoming a virtual tollbooth for the region. The conversion of the city into the center of the Vice-royalty of the River Plate legitimized much of the contraband that took place, but it also sowed the seeds for the rivalry that would emerge after the region gained its independence from Spain. The first half century of the nation's history was marked by the constant struggle between Buenos Aires and the provinces. Although the conflict would ultimately be resolved in a string of military engagements, the contest would become a permanent feature of the political background. The dominant role of Buenos Aires is relatively unique for Latin America. Most of the other countries in the region have two or more cities that vie for the control of the nation. The competition between Rio de Janeiro and Sao Paulo, for example, was a steady feature of Brazil's political history. The tug of war between Quito and Guayaquil shaped Ecuador's development. The jealousy between Bogota and Medellin defined many of the policy decisions that were taken in Colombia. However, Buenos Aires never had a rival that matched its power and prestige. With more than 40 percent of the country's population living in Buenos Aires, it outclassed all of the other provinces and urban centers. Even secondary cities such as Rosario, Santa Fe, and Cordoba never came close to approaching the resources and wealth it enjoyed. Consequently, Buenos Aires could play a hegemonic role. However, the port city could never stand up to the amalgamation of the provinces. Therefore, the political stability of the country is based on the equitable sharing of resources between Buenos Aires and the provinces.

The second role that the geography of Argentina played was in the shaping of the national leader. The ruggedness of the land imbued the inhabitants with a sense of savagery, thus allowing the most ruthless individuals to thrive. It molded the nature of the gauchos who roamed the pampas, as well as the caudillos that provided a semblance of law and order. The inherent barbarism of the Argentine leader was a theme picked up by Sarmiento and vilified in his book, *Facundo*. The natural tendency toward autocracy and the deep desire for civilization caused one of the permanent psychological conflicts of Argentine society. Not only have strong leaders been successful; the population pines for them. At the same time, Argentines want to be recognized for their Western values and traditions. From the Beaux-Arts architectural style of Buenos Aires to the European rhythms embedded in tangos to the European regional cuisines that make up the mainstay of the local diet, Argentines reject Latin American culture. Yet, their political system is one of the most primitive of the region. The immense centralization of power in individuals rather than institutions produced an arbitrary approach that subsisted on populism and clientelism. Indeed, the focus on individual whims rather than institutional rules produced a pattern of sudden shifts and reversals that never allowed the country to maximize its potential.

The penchant for strong leadership suppressed the creation of independent institutions that could provide checks and balances. On the contrary, ever since the days of Rosas there has been a reliance on special powers or decrees by those in power. This has reduced the need to consult with any legislative assembly. This pattern has consistently been repeated by civilian and military governments. Even the superpowers that were granted to Cavallo to deal with the debt crisis of 2001 and Fernandez's unilateral decision in 2008 to nationalize the pension funds testified to the prevalence of an authoritarian style. Indeed, the strong nature of the Argentine leader explains the constant reiteration of presidents with military backgrounds. From Rosas to Mitre to Roca to Peron, Argentines always have preferred soldiers as their leaders. Unfortunately, mild-mannered leaders, such as Rivadavia, Frondizi, Illia, and de la Rua were not allowed to serve their full terms in office.

The centralization of power lent itself to the use of political machines that exchanged patronage for political support. They were permanent features of the national landscape. It did not matter whether this was done by the right or the left. The conservative factions divided the spoils of the Campaign of the Desert among themselves. They shared lucrative contracts among one another during the Age of Infamy. Likewise, the left used its position to increase benefits for the poor in exchange for blind loyalty. The political machines also deployed militant arms, such as the Mazorca, the Asociacion del Trabajo, and the piqueteros to enforce discipline, devotion, and order. The most perfected political machine was established by Juan Domingo Peron. Using a corporatist framework, the Peronist organization allowed the leadership to shower economic favors in return for political allegiance. Yet, in time, it became apparent that the machine had supplanted the individual. This was a notion that was picked by Lonardi when he developed the slogan "Peronism without Peron." The prominence of the machine could explain why some of the country's most prominent leaders were easily swept from power even though the apparatus remained in place. Two good examples were the defeat of Rosas at Caseros and the coup against Peron. Both individuals were overwhelmingly dominant. Yet, both were easily swept aside without any popular backlash after they lost their support due to arrogance and insolence.

The geographic and political characteristics of Argentina have been permanent features since its inception. Therefore, the fact that the country enjoyed an unprecedented era of prosperity at the start of the twentieth century was due to external factors rather than internal decisions. Likewise, the turn of events during the latter half of the twentieth century was due to a sharp deterioration in the terms of trade rather than bad policy choices. The country's heavy reliance on its areas of comparative advantage and its individualistic forms of government has accentuated the amplitude of the business cycle. This has had nothing to do with who colonized Argentina or what nationalities immigrated there.

In order to smooth the oscillations, Argentina must find ways to increase the value-added content of its areas of relative strength. To that end, the nation is well prepared for the opportunities that lie on the horizon. With the growing prosperity that is appearing across much of the developing world, it is well positioned to convert its abundant water resources into food products that will be needed to meet expanding dietary needs. The strong rains that blanket the country, the deep rivers, the large aquifers, and vast ice fields provide an important buffer to counter the climatic changes that are challenging other parts of the globe. Argentina is also enhancing the value-added component of its agricultural production by developing new technologies, products, and services. Likewise, the development of the Vaca Muerta gas/oil fields will catapult the country into the top tier of the energy-producing world. With much of the infrastructure already in place to exploit and transport the hydrocarbons that will be extracted, it will benefit from the new fracking technologies that are being developed. All of these factors confirm that geography was the main factor that dictated the Land of Silver's last two hundred years, and geography will determine its future.

Bibliography

Aldo Ferrer. *La Economía Argentina: Desde sus Orígenes hasta los Principios del Siglo XXI*. Buenos Aires: Fondo de Cultura Económica, 2004.

Bocco, Arnaldo. *Privatizaciones: Restructuración del Estado y de la Sociedad.* Buenos Aires: Ediciones Letra Buena, 1991.

Bordo, Michael D. and Roberto Cortés Conde. *Transferring Wealth and Power from the Old to the New World: Monetary and Fiscal Institutions in the 17th through the 19th Centuries.* Cambridge: Cambridge University Press, 2001.

Brennan, James and Marcelo Rougier. *The Politics of National Capitalism: Peronism and the Argentine Bourgeoisie, 1946-1976.* University Park: Pennsylvania State University Press, 2009.

Bruno, Eugenio Andrea. *El Default y la Reestructacion de la Deuda.* Buenos Aires: Nueva Mayoría, 2004.

Campobassi, José. *Sarmiento y Mitre: Hombres de Mayo y Caseros.* Buenos Aires: Editorial Losada, 1952.

Cepeda, Carlos Ramil. *Crisis de una Burguesía Dependiente: Balance Económico de la "Revolución Argentina" 1966-1971*. Buenos Aires: Edición La Rosa Blindada, 1972.

Collier, Ruth Berins and David Collier. *Shaping the Political Arena: Critical Junctures, the Labor Movement, and Regime Dynamics in Latin America*. Princeton: Princeton University Press, 1991.

Conesa, Eduardo. *Que Pasa en la Economía Argentina*. Buenos Aires: Ediciones Macchi, 2000.

Cortes Conde, Roberto. *Progreso y Declinacion de la Economia Argentina*. Buenos Aires: Fondo de la Cultura Economica, 1998.

Cortes Conde, Roberto. *The First Stages of Modernization in Spanish America*. New York: Harper & Row, 1974.

Economy, Elizabeth. "China's Growing Water Crisis," *World Politics Review*, August 9, 2011.

Fraga, Rosendo. *Contexto Político y Privatizaciones en la Argentina*. Buenos Aires: Centro de Estudios Union Para la Nueva Mayoría, 1994.

Garner, William. *The Chaco Dispute*. Washington, D.C.: Public Affairs Press, 1966.

Grover, Velma. *Water: A Source of Conflict or Cooperation*. Enfield: Science Publishers, 2007.

Horowitz, Joel. *Argentine Unions, the State and the Rise of Peronism*. Berkeley: University of California Press, 1990.

Horowitz, Joel. *Argentina's Radical Party and Popular Mobilization, 1916-1930*. University Park: Pennsylvania State University Press, 2008.

James, Daniel. *Resistance and Integration: Peronism and the Argentine Working Class, 1946-1976*. Cambridge: Cambridge University Press, 1988.

Jeffrey, William. *Mitre and Argentina.* New York: Library Publisher, 1952.

Lamas, Daniel Rodríguez. *La Revolución Libertadora.* Buenos Aires: Centro Editor de América Latina, 1985.

Lebedinsky, Mauricio. *Sarmiento, Más alla de la Educacion.* Buenos Aires: Capital Intelectual, 2009.

Lewis, Collin. *British Railways in Argentina 1857-1914.* London: University of London, 1983.

Luna, Felix. *Conflictos en la Argentina Prospera.* Buenos Aires: Editorial Planeta, 2000.

Margheritis, Ana. *Ajuste y Reforma En Argentina (1989-1995).* Buenos Aires: Nuevohacer, 1999.

Marx, Karl and Frederic Engels. *The Communist Manifesto.* London: William Reeves Bookseller, 1888.

Molano, Walter. *The Logic of Privatization.* Westport: Greenwood Press, 1997.

O'Neill, James. *Building Better Global Economic BRICs.* Goldman Sachs, 2001.

Orszag, Peter. "Why We Care About the Price of Water in China," *Bloomberg Magazine*, July 6, 2011).

Osvaldo, Bayer. *Patagonia Rebelde.* México, D.F.: Editorial Nueva Imagen, 1980.

Rock, David. *Argentina 1516-1987.* Los Angeles: University of California Press, 1987.

Rock, David. *Politics in Argentina 1890-1930: The Rise and Fall of Radicalism.* Cambridge: Cambridge University Press, 1975.

Santa Cruz , Juan Manuel. *Ferrocarriles Argentinos.* Buenos Aires: Facultad de Ciencias Economicas, Comerciales y Politicas, 1966.

Sarmiento, Domingo Faustino. *Civilization and Barbarism,* trans. Kathleen Ross Berkeley: University of California Press, 2003.

Schmitter, Philippe C. and Gerhard Lehmbruch, *Trends towards corporatist intermediation.* London: Sage Publications, 1979.

Solanet, Manuel. *La hiperinflación del 89.* Buenos Aires: Lumiere, 2006.

Solberg, Carl. *Oil and Nationalism in Argentina.* Stanford: Stanford University Press, 1979.

Szusterman, Celia. *Frondizi and the Politics of Developmentalism in Argentina, 1955-62.* London: The Macmillan Press, 1993.

Terragno, Rodolfo. *Privatizaciones en la Argentina.* Buenos Aires: Fundacion Omega Seguros, 2000.

Villavicencio, Susana. *Sarmiento y La Nacion Civica.* Buenos Aires: Universidad de Buenos Aires, 2008.

Wesson, Robert. *U.S. Influence in Latin America in the 1980s.* Stanford: Hoover Institute Press, 1982.

Whitfield, Susan with Ursula Sims-Williams, eds. *The Silk Route: Trade, Travel, War and Faith.* London: British Library, 2004

Willis, Bailey. *Northern Patagonia: Character and Resources.* Buenos Aires: Ministry of Public Works, 1914.

World Bank. "Progress in Privatization in Developing Countries," *Global Development Finance.* Washington: World Bank, 2001.

Zook, David. *The Conduct of the Chaco War.* New Haven: Bookman Associates, 1960.

Index

Made in the USA
Charleston, SC
05 November 2013